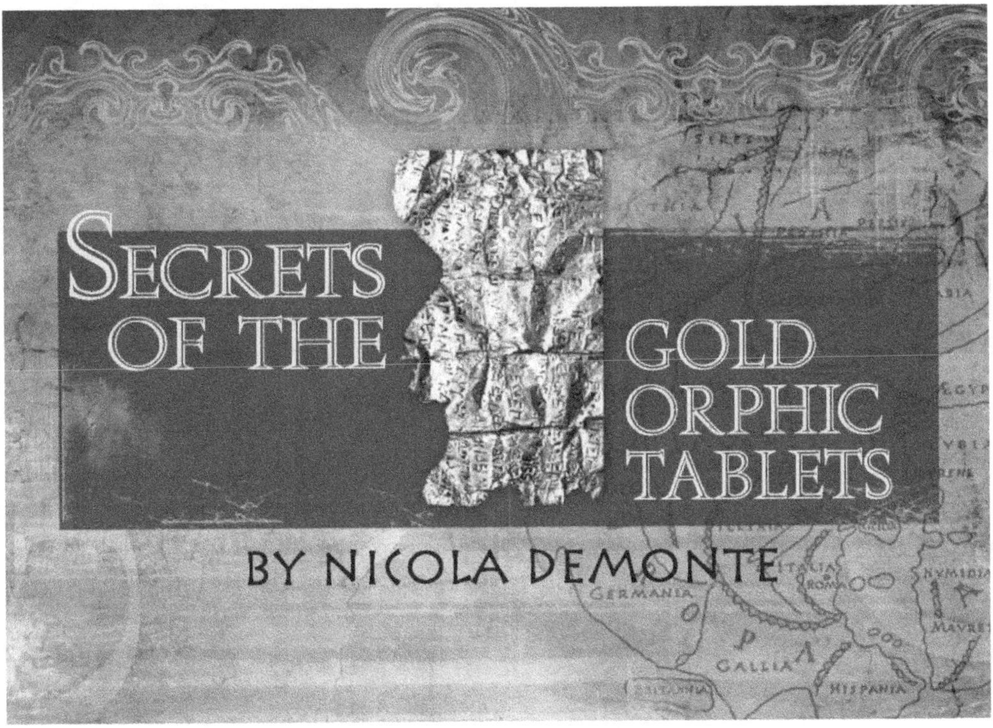

SECRETS OF THE GOLD ORPHIC TABLETS

BY NICOLA DEMONTE

Secrets of the Gold Orphic Tablets

ISBN-13: 978-1456557669
ISBN-10: 1456557661

I would like to thank my family, friends and colleagues for their support and encouragement throughout the years, and to Flora Caputo for designing the beautiful book cover.

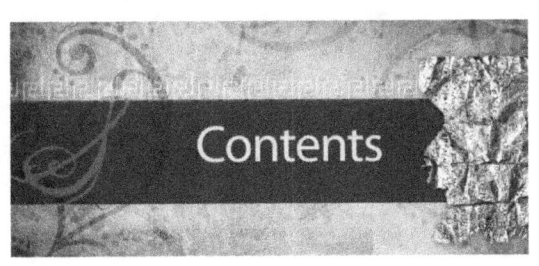

Contents

Chapter 1

Orpheus was a legendary poet, musician, and prophet of classical mythology. The Sixth century B.C. sculptured panels at the Sikyonian Treasury of Delphi depicts the Argonauts' myth and a bearded Orpheus playing his lyre on the ship of the Argo. Apollo, the god of song, sent Orpheus to Jason and the Argonauts. Equipped with the lyre as a weapon and instrument to command the rowers, Orpheus fought the sea creatures. Pindar writes that Orpheus is "the father of songs" who perfected the lyre and could charm animals, fish, rocks, and trees. Apollodorus and Pindar cite Orpheus as a historical figure, naming him to be the son of Oeagrus, a Thracian king.

Greek mythology names Apollo as his father, and his mother, the muse Calliope. In the *Argonautica*, a Greek poem written by Apollonius Rhodius in the 3rd century BC, Orpheus accompanies Jason and the Argonauts to retrieve the Golden Fleece, and, using his magical abilities to play his lyre, enchants the dangerous Sirens, allowing the sailors to pass unharmed. Orpheus was no average poet or musician, but a magician with powers to animate inanimate objects, as well as to and influence deities, mythical creatures, and humans. His songs celebrated the creation of the universe, the clash of the Titans and Zeus. Orpheus has a hand in the cult of Rhea, with drums that set a stage for musical and dance performances.

In the *Argonautica*, Orpheus sings a hymn and declares sacrificial rites upon the arrival of Jason and company to the isle of Thynias:

"Come, let us name the sacred island of Apollo Heoius, because he appeared at dawn to us all as he passed by, and let us set up an altar on the shore and sacrifice whatever is at hand.

When the Argonauts are stranded on an island, Orpheus builds an altar to Apollo and sings a hymn in honor of the god. During the voyage home, the Argonauts search for a spring to quench their thirst, encountering nymphs who are transformed into dust and earth. Orpheus sings to the nymphs, and asks for water:

The women instantly turned to dust and earth there on the spot. Orpheus recognized the divine portent and for his comrades' sake sought to comfort the nymphs with prayers. "O goddesses beautiful and kind, be gracious, O queens whether you are counted among the heavenly goddesses or those under the earth, or are called solitary nymphs, come, O nymphs, holy offspring of Ocean, and appear before our longing eyes and show us either some flower of water from a rock or some sacred stream gushing from the ground, goddesses, with which we may relieve our endlessly burning thirst.
Apollonius, The Argonauts. (pp. 1408-1418).

The "'burning thirst" Orpheus desires is reincarnation after death. The Greek religious tradition that honored the rebirth of one's soul or metempsychosis (μετεμψύχωσις) began in 1200 BCE with the Pre-Socratic and later philosophers. Phereciydes of Syros, Pythagoras, Plato, and Socrates are some of the philosophers who started conversations where the idea of rebirth was introduced.

The Latin meaning of reincarnation is "entering the flesh again," and was popularized by the Greek dramatist Menander, the satirist Lucian of Samosata, and the father of Roman poetry, Quintus Ennius. Virgil writes about the idea of rebirth in the sixth book of the *Aeneid*.

The Central Argument

One of the central arguments and problematic issues surrounding "Orphic" texts remains whether they can be tied to a specific ritual tradition that began with the cult of Orpheus. An Orphic could be identified as any individual who believed that Orpheus' teachings could bring them to truth and immortality. Rituals and beliefs could include (but were not limited to) the worship of Dionysus, Persephone / Demeter, Zeus and the sun. At the center of this teaching was the belief that the soul had reincarnated into various forms (animals, plants, humans) but that its potential was to become immortal, and therefore, not be re-born. Orphics may have also embraced such actions as vegetarianism, since an animal would naturally contain the soul from a past life.[1] Maintaining purity of the soul was necessary to achieve immortality, so any contact with animal meat would have had serious repercussions in the afterlife. Previous attempts to prove a doctrine of metempsychosis relied upon the teachings of the Philosopher Empedocles (477 B.C. – 432 B.C.) who wrote on the reincarnation of souls into animal forms.[2] Before the discovery of the gold lamellae, there was no evidence that Orphics had believed or practiced rituals of immortalization. Following the publications of more than 20 lamellae, we are beginning to unshed the mysteries of reincarnation and the amulets that were believed to counteract rebirth. What do the burial contents of Orphic/Dionysiac cults tell us about their beliefs regarding the reincarnation of the soul? Based on the gold lamellae found at various locations throughout Magna Graecia, Thessaly, Crete and Scythia, we are able to piece together a complex network of "Orphic" beliefs. The sacred knowledge interspersed in ritual tradition of these groups have come down to us in the curious gold lamellae or golden "leaves", the Derveni Papyrus and the bone plates from Olbia. Orpheus is said to have published the first works on botany, which included the discovery of a plant called polium.[3] These plants and herbs were to be administered through fumigations as a cure for illness or as an

---

[1] Empedocles, "The Extant Fragments," Trans. & Ed. M. R. Wright (London: Bristol Classical Press, 1995) Fr. 120(139): pp. 144 and 284.
[2] Empedocles, Περὴ "Φύσεως and Καθαρμο–," Trans. Henry W. Johnstone, Jr. (Bryn Mawr, PA: Bryn Mawr Commentaries, 1985) 30 and 43.
[3] Pliny, "Natural History XXIV-XXVII," Trans. W. H. S. Jones (Cambridge, Massachusetts: Harvard University Press, 2001) 145.

aphrodisiac.[4] Orpheus's role as a botanist may explain why a lamella was fashioned as a leaf or plant. The Latin name for *lamella*, or thin metal plate, often refers to the Greek amulets or talismans made from gold, silver, lead, or iron. Accompanying text and/or symbols are then engraved and worn either as a protective device (gold and silver) or, in the case of malicious or demonic magic, lead or iron. In the case examples soon to be discussed, gold is meant to protect the soul against the terrors of the afterlife. Walter Burkert has worked through some of the methodological and interpretive problems in reconstructing "Orphic ideas", citing the difficulty in not knowing the true author of these lamellae.[5] Regarding the cohesive nature of the Orphic cult, Burkert explains:

> "The controversies about Orphism focus on the extent to which it can be seen as a unified spiritual movement, whether based on the anthropogonic Dionysos myth or on the doctrine of immortality and transmigration of souls."[6]

More specifically, the question of metempsychosis, the belief that the soul reincarnates into different bodies, has been a particular concern in modern literature. Burkert defines Orphic metempsychosis within the realm of Dionysiac "cultic ecstasy" or "βαχXεύειν,"[7] a raising of consciousness in which death is overcome. The Orphics appeared to be a

---

[4] Pliny, "Natural History XX-XXIII," Trans. W. H. S. Jones (Cambridge, Massachusetts: Harvard University Press, 1999) 21.
[5] Walter Burkert, "Orphism and Bacchic Mysteries: New Evidence and Old Problems of Interpretation," in *Protocol of the 28th Colloquy of the Center for Hermeneutical Studies in Hellenistic and Modern Culture*, ed. Wilhelm Wuellner (Berkeley: Center for Hermeneutical Studies, 1977) 1-8. Burkert contends that the Orphic mystery cults may have incorporated beliefs from the traditions of Eleusis, Bacchus, and Pythagoras. The common characteristics among them dealt with purification of the soul, afterlife concerns and transformation through ritual.

[6] Walter Burkert, "Greek Religion, " (Massachusetts: Harvard University Press, 1998) 297.
[7] Walter Burkert, "Orphism and Bacchic Mysteries: New Evidence and Old Problems of Interpretation," 4.

literary group and therefore used tools like papyri and lamellae in order to achieve

ecstasy and esoteric knowledge. Let us the consider the main question of this thesis: Did

these Orphic lamellae serve a ritual function to protect the soul from reincarnation?

The Written Tradition

This practice of placing papyri and gold tablets among initiates may be viewed in

its post-mortem context: it is a testament to the Orphic belief that memory is a vehicle

toward metempsychosis and purification of the soul. Preserving memory, or the ability of

one to recall past events represents an important aspect in Orphic initiations; this will

allow the soul to recall past events, know what he/she has done wrong, and subsequently

journey toward the path of the immortals. In preparation of one's death, one presumably

practiced the various procedures by reading the oracles of Orpheus and gaining insight

into their meaning. With respect to the books reportedly written by Orpheus, Plato

contends that:

πείθντες οὐ μῷνον ἠδιώτας
ἀλλά καὴ πῷλεις

"And these books they use in
their ritual."[8]

Socrates makes clear that such books are helpful in purifying souls of any sins

committed. The discussion between the philosophers in this passage does not explain the

actual content of the books, but it does provide us with an important clue regarding the

gold lamellae. Socrates continues his discussion by noting a second classification apart

from the standard books these priests carry from city to city:

---

[8] Plato, "The Republic: Books I-V," Trans. Paul Shorey (Cambridge, Massachusetts: Harvard University Press, 1999) 134 and 135, respectively.

ἀδικημάτων διαθυσών καὴ παιδιας Εδονών εὴσὴ
μάν ᾳτι ζώσιν, εὴσὴ δά καὴ τελευτΕσασιν, ᾳς δΕ
τελετάς καλούσιν, αἳ τών έκε κακών ἀπολύουσιν
Εμας, μΕ θύσαντας δά δεινα περιμάνει.

"There are also special rites for the defunct, which
they call functions, that deliver us from evils in that
other world, while terrible things await those who
have neglected to sacrifice."[9]

The Orphic/Bacchic magical formularies in the gold tablets were meant to be

secret. First, only an experienced priest could carry out the prescribed text as a funerary

hymn to the deceased. Second, the individual who passed on would presumably have

needed training in the "Orphic" arts in preparation for the afterlife journey. Beginning in

the fourth century B.C. , those *amystēriastos*[10] who were uninitiated, and thus ignorant of

ritual and theological teachings, would have difficulty in procuring these gold tablets.

A Theory of Metempsychosis

---

[9] Plato, "The Republic: Books I-V," 134 and 135, respectively. It is quite possible that
"special" rites refer to the gold leaves which do in fact address the "evils" in Hades.
These "functions" may reference the symbols or passwords that the initiate would have to
use to avoid rebirth (Tablets B11 and Ph). More on these passwords will be discussed in
the following chapters. Special rites, according to Socrates, suggests rituals and amulets
that were reserved for certain individuals and not accessible to the general public.

[10] For a discussion in which uninitiated or *amystēriastos* are excluded from the secret
names see Hans Dieter Betz, "The Formation of Authoritative Tradition in the Greek
Magical Papyri," *Jewish and Christian Self-Definition: Volume Three, Self-Definition in
the Graeco-Roman World.* (London: SCM Press, 1982) 167. It also appears that even
initiates who were inducted into the mysteries could be excluded from immortality if they
chose to "disobey" the secrect *apokryphōi* tradition. For an example of this secret oath,
see also the five year period of silence for Pythagorean neophytes (Iamblichus, vit. Pyth,
On the Pythagôrean Life, trans. Gillian Clark (Liverpool: Liverpool University Press,
1989) p. 32.

The primary questions I shall investigate are: What do the Orphic testimonia reveal about the need for *gnōsis*[11] or developing a hidden word system to purify the soul as a means to avoid metempsychosis? Various lamellae contain secret names and passwords that must either be written or spoken before the guardians of Hades (Lamellae B1, B11, PH, etc).[12] Deciphering their nature, meaning, and origin, will help us understand the "mechanics" of ritual formulary. Furthermore, the Orphic followers believed that:

1) reincarnation or metempsychosis was a lower existence equated with evil,

2) reincarnation could only be avoided by gaining *gnōsis* (knowledge), and

3) the gold lamellae served as amulets to protect the soul from being re-born.

The gold tablets re-create a symbolic language for Orphic followers (*teletai*) to achieve immortality in the afterlife. Teletai would use these gold tablets as instruction manuals, road maps that help them navigate the underworld. Based on these amulets, did the Orphics believe in reincarnation, and if so, how could memorization of formulas avoid rebirth? How can writing itself be viewed as a symbolic system, whereby esoteric knowledge is inscribed on materials like gold, bronze, pottery, stone, papyri, or bone? In excavations of these burial tombs, what archaeological data confirms an Orphic cult?

---

[11] In his work *Stromata* or "Miscellanies", Clement of Alexandria, a primary source on the Greek mystery religions and cults consistently describes *gnōsis* as "knowledge". The natural soul must undergo serious training. First, it must learn certain things, thus acquiring knowledge and then act though impulse. *Gnōsis* is not, according to Clement, something that men are born with, but a "mystic habit" or disposition that demands disciplined training. For the training of *gnōsis* among initiates, see Clement of Alexandria, *Extracts from the Writings of Clement of Alexandria* (New York: John Lane, 1905) 31-38.

[12] See Chapter 3 for a discussion of the lamellae classification.

I hypothesize that the Orphic texts found on the gold leaves or lamellae, served a ritual and post-mortem function in Greek and Roman burial customs starting in the fourth century B.C. Believing that the lamella would ensure an immortal existence, the individual wore it either before and/or after death. If the individual followed the directions correctly than he/she would walk among other initiates. Should the amulet be discarded or its contents ignored, then the soul would endure punishment and rebirth. The symbolic nature of the gold lamellae functioned as: 1) allegorical formularies for the initiate to remember past lives; For example, the lamellae contain narratives of Dionysus that symbolize the death and immortalization of the soul and is connected with Persephone's grief and Zeus' wraith; 2) a ritual "apparatus" or amulet, a tool used in Orphic funerary rites. Inscription of formulas served to re-enact legends as a means to communicate with a divinity; 3) a magical amulet to train the memory of the *teletai*. In tablets B1 and B2 from Petelia, Italy and Pharsalos, Thessaly (400 B.C. to 320 B.C.) the soul is directed toward the lake of Memory, while in tablet A5 from Rome (260 A.D.), Caecilia Secundina (the *teletai* who is named in the lamella) claims the gift of memory. Furthermore, the formularies in these amulets formed a consistent body of beliefs that would help purify the dead. An analysis of the gold tablets and Derveni papyrus (PDERV) will show how this process of purification was to be enacted: the encoded formulary was to activate the soul's memory to remember any past transgressions and dispositions that kept him in the wheel of birth and death. Evidence of this purification can be found in the following formulas: "Pure I come from the pure" (tablets A1, A2, A3, A5),[13] the association of the soul with a divine lineage (tablets A5, B1, B2, B3, B4, B5,

---

[13] R. Edmonds, *Roads Not Taken: Explorations of the 'Orphic' Gold Tablets*

B6, B7, B8, B9, B10, B11),[14] references to rebirth (tablets A4, A5, P1, P2, B10, B11),[15] and Orpheus delivering riddles for "pure" initiates (PDERV, Col. VII, IX, X, XIII, XVIII, XX).[16] A summary analysis and case-by-case study of the lamellae and Derveni Papyrus will support an Orphic belief in reincarnation. Examples like the Petelia lamella also show the extent they were used for everyday adornment on necklaces, possibly functioning as jewelry. The gold foil was then rolled up and placed inside the capsule, hidden to others and containing the magical formulary. This formed a literary / ritualistic function since it was to be read by the individual during the afterlife journey. Most of the gold foils have been folded, unfolded, creased and show signs of cracking. It appears that such items were in use even before the person's burial.

(Unpublished transcript from the Chicago Humanities Institute, University of Chicago, 1997). Received by Prof. Albert Henrichs, spring 2003. 13-14.

[14] Edmonds, 14-18.

[15] Edmonds, 14, 17-18.

[16] Andre Laks & Glenn W. Most "A Provisional Translation of the Derveni Papyrus". In: *Studies on the Derveni Papyrus*. (Oxford: Clarendon Press, 1997) 12-22.

Chapter 2

Definition of Terms

This book is operating under two definitions:

"Orphism": an ancient Thracian mystery religion, founded upon the teachings of the poet Orpheus, with beliefs in reincarnation, purity of the soul, and the use of ritual formularies to achieve immortality of the soul.

"Metempsychosis": reincarnation or transmigration of the soul, a re-birth of the individual into another human body, animal or plant form.

Orphic Legends

Perhaps no other musician and poet from antiquity has captured man's imagination as Orpheus has. Whether real or mythical, his ability to mesmerize animals and enchant deities has strengthened his reputation as a seer,[17] diviner, magician, musician, poet, prophet and philosopher.[18] The varying accounts regarding Orpheus' travels provide a fascinating look into the origin of Greek mystery cults. While the Orphic cult and its practices were believed to have originated from Thrace and Samothrace,[19] both Diodorus of Sicily and Herodotus trace the origins back to Egypt. Their accounts also tell of Orpheus' travels to Egypt but provide no exact date.

---

[17] Pliny, "Natural History III-VII," Trans. H. Rackham (Cambridge, Massachusetts: Harvard University Press, 1999) 643.

[18] Julian, "The Works of the Emperor Julian: Vol. II," Trans. Wilmer Cave Wright (Cambridge, Massachusetts: Harvard University Press, 1969) 99.

[19] Diodorus of Sicily. Book II. Trans. C. H. Oldfather (Cambridge, Massachusetts: Harvard University Press, 1933) 477 and 495.

Herodotus (Book II) writes of a prohibition against wearing wool in temples or being buried with this cloth.[20] Herodotus describes these rites as originating from the Egyptians and Pythagoreans, having later been adapted by the cults of Orpheus and Bacchus. In another account by Diodorus of Sicily, Orpheus visits Egypt and partakes in the mysteries of Dionysus.[21] After having experienced these rites, Orpheus discovers Zeus and Semele as the parents of Dionysus and Osiris and regards Thebes as the birthplace of the child-god.[22] In speaking of Osiris, Orpheus claims:

το῀νεκῷ μιν καλῆουσι Φῶνητῷ τε καῆ Διἀνυσον.

"And this is why men call him Shining One and Dionysus.[23]

Dionysus and the Afterlife

Dionysus and Osiris (believed by Orpheus and others to be the same god) achieved immortality through death and rebirth, sharing similar ideals in the mythology of Greece and Egypt. Having been dismembered and killed, their bodies were brought back to life by the female deities Isis and Athena. It is no surprise then, that Orpheus

---

[20] Herodotus, "Books I-II," Trans. A. D. Godley (Cambridge, Massachusetts: Harvard University Press, 1996) 367. This prohibition against wearing wool may reflect a belief in reincarnation, in which the soul of the animal is believed to be housed in the wool.

[21] Diodorus of Sicily, "I: Books I and II, 1-34," Trans. C. H. Oldfather (Cambridge, Massachusetts: Harvard University Press, 1933) 73.

[22] Diodorus of Sicily, 73 & 327. Since Dionysus was born of Semele, daughter of an Egyptian named Cadmus, Osiris, who is also born from the same mother is believed to be the same god as Dionysus. Hence, Orpheus regards Osiris as the same god and transfers his birth to Thebes, incorporating him as the god Dionysus to be worshipped by the Greeks; the same comparison also being made of Demeter and Isis.

[23] Diodorus of Sicily, 38 & 39, respectively.

would have chosen these two gods to represent the mystic rites concerning the afterlife. Orpheus was so enamored by Egyptian funeral customs that he transferred many of these practices into those found in Greece. One of these rites concerns the punishment of the unrighteous in Hades and the fields of the Righteous[24] where only pure souls are allowed to enter (elements found in tablets A1-A4, Ph, B10 and B11). Following Diodorus' discussion of Egyptian embalming techniques and the travel of the Egyptian soul across the lake in the afterlife, he writes that during ancient times Orpheus incorporated Egyptian funerary beliefs and customs to explain his own travels in Hades.[25] According to two separate accounts by Diodorus (which seem to contradict one another), there is no truth to Orpheus' Thracian descent to Hades, for it never really happened (Book I). Instead, Diodorus explains that Orpheus concocted the story by mixing elements of Egyptian funerary practices with those of his own imagination. In contrast to Book I, Book IV by Diodorus explains that Orpheus had descended into Hades where he persuaded Persephone and Hades to release his wife.[26] In any event, Diodorus (Book I and IV) provides the link between Orphic / Bacchic orgiastic rituals and the Egyptian belief regarding an immortal soul.

Genealogy

The fact that over twenty-one tablets and oracular texts have been attributed to the poet from Thrace perhaps shows the importance of Orphic belief and practice in Greek religion. Secret names as delineated in the *gnōsis* of the tablets and papyri are often

---

[24] Diodorus of Sicily, Book I, 327.
[25] Diodorus of Sicily, Book I, 315.
[26] Diodorus of Sicily. Book II. Trans. C. H. Oldfather (Cambridge, Massachusetts: Harvard University Press, 1933) 425.

written as if Orpheus had disclosed them to the initiate in a state of supreme revelation whereby beliefs in the afterlife, salvation of the soul, and creation of the universe are transmitted in formulae. The Orphic tradition of writing down these magical systems, most notably in burial contexts, was not so as to create a compendium of cultic knowledge, but to record the teachings of Orpheus for ritual purposes of avoiding reincarnation. One particular formula states "as the diviner Orpheus handed it down through his book Parastichis."[27] We may gain a better understanding of Orpheus by tracing the stories of his divine lineage; writers like Pindar and Plato have elaborated on his immortal parents since it bestowed an aura of authority and respect upon the famous poet. In a differing account, Pliny does not mention an immortal lineage but instead supports Orpheus' Thracian ancestry from the Moriseni and Sithoni of the Black Sea.[28] Clement of Alexandria and Diodorus of Sicily[29] write of a man named Oeagrus as the father of Orpheus, with mention of the latter as a "Thracian."[30] We see the importance of documenting oracles in a red-figure kylix (Fig.1) in which a decapitated Orpheus is speaking to a seated youth. On the right stands Apollo[31] holding a laurel staff in his left hand. The seated youth sits with tablet and stylus as if recording the details of the

[27] Betz, H.D., 166.

[28] Pliny, "Natural History III-VII," Trans. H. Rackham (Cambridge, Massachusetts: Harvard University Press, 1999) 149.

[29] Diodorus of Sicily. Book II. Trans. C. H. Oldfather (Cambridge, Massachusetts: Harvard University Press, 1933) 301. Diodorus interestingly claims that Orpheus had learned the mysteries and rites from his father, Oeagrus.

[30] Clement of Alexandria, "Exhortation to the Greeks and The Rich Man's Salvation to the Newly Baptized," Trans. G.W. Butterworth. Ed. G.P. Goold (Cambridge, Massachusetts: Harvard University Press, 1999) 167.

oracle.[32] The outstretched arm of Apollo either lends authority to the oracle or challenges

the magical prose flowing from the head of Orpheus. In Pindar's ode to the *Pythian*

games (circa 470 B.C.), he states that:

ἐξ Ἀπολλωνος sέφρμιγκτάs ἀοιδάν πατΕρ
ημολεν, εὐα–νητοs Ὀρφεύs

"And from Apollo came the father of songs,
the widely praised minstrel Orpheus."[33]

These so-called scribes shown in the kylix above, may have worked in private,

recording previous manuscripts, or worked from an oral tradition. In any event, we

should not automatically assume that such individuals were the wandering priests

documented by Plato. Even though Plato is critical of the Orphic priests who sell charms

for purification of the soul in the afterlife, he documents the tradition of knowledge in the

mysteries:

βίβλων δὰ ἇμαδον παρέχονται Μουσα–ου κὰη Ὀρ-
φέωs, Σελήs τε κὰη Μουσών ἐγγὰνων, ὡs φασι,
καθ' ἇs θυηπολοῦσι

"And they produce a bushel of books of Musaeus and
Orpheus, the offspring of the Moon and of the
Muses, as they affirm."[34]

---

[32] *Lexicon Iconographicum Mythologiae Classicae: VII.* Zurich: ArtemisVerlag, 1994.
No. 70, p. 88. What was written on this tablet we shall not know. The composition and
transcription of the oracle is shrouded in mystery and purportedly intended for the
Orphikoi, Bacchoi, and members of secret cults. Is this meant to reference a golden
lamella or a larger manuscript that would have been read by the itinerant priests?

[33] Pindar, "Olympian Odes and Pythian Odes I. Ed. and Trans. William H. Race.
(Cambridge, Massachusetts: Harvard University Press, 1997) 282 and 283, respectively.
[34] Plato, "The Republic: Books I-V," Trans. Paul Shorey (Cambridge, Massachusetts:
Harvard University Press, 1999) 134 and 135, respectively.

Tracing the lineage of Orpheus to the moon goddess is important, since it leads us to

Diana or Luna/(Selene in the Greek tradition), sister of Helios and Apollo; she causes

darkness each evening while riding her chariot, and consorts with nymphs and creatures

of the night. Polar opposites, as in the Lunar/Solar context, are important attributes in

Orphic cosmogony[35]; one god/goddess is not complete without the other. They symbolize

the chthonic/primal forces from that dark void (night) that was once cosmos. The Orphic

preoccupation with one's immortal ancestors served to remind them that mortality could

be overcome: the gold leaves allow the mendicant to mimetically re-enact the death of

Dionysus through his/her own death; purification is dependent on the initiate's

identification with the fallen child-king. Evidence of this can be found in the death and

rebirth of "Bacchios" (Tablets P1, P2), and the "Male child of the thyrsos" (Pherai

Tablet, Ph of unknown date). [36] Night is the all-encompassing darkness that existed from

the beginning of creation; she is the 'nurse' who teaches (PDERV Col. X),[37] the source

of oracles and moral advice (PDERV Col. XI),[38] and one who is subservient to Zeus

(PDERV Col. XIII).[39] It will be shown that the celestial heavens, and the planetary

systems (in conjunction with the Olympian and chthonic deities) played important roles

---

[35] Walter Burkert, "Greek Religion," 296. While the tradition of Greek cosmogony centered on "Ouranos-Kronos-Zeus" (p. 296) as the first creators of man, Burkert emphasizes how the Derveni Papyrus shifted the focus by extending this genealogy even further beyond Hesiod's *Theogony*; what is essentially named "Orphic" is one that recognizes Night or Chaos as the beginning of creation.

[36] Edmonds, p 14 and 18, respectively.

[37] Laks and Most, 13.

[38] Laks and Most, 14.

[39] Laks and Most, 14-15.

in Orphic cosmogonic beliefs. These chthonic deities, according to the tablets and the

Derveni papyrus, used both violence and sexual deviancy to propagate both immortals

and mortals. This idea of sexual deviancy and subjugation through violence will prove

fruitful to our understanding of how metempsychosis was perceived and ritualized among

these mystery traditions.

Evidence regarding a Theory of Metempsychosis

This present hypothesis (Pages 7-8) challenges the contention by Larry Alderink

that "We find, therefore, little evidence (with the exception of Plato's statement in the

Meno) to indicate that Orphism included a theory of metempsychosis."[40] Further

commentaries like the one proposed by Ivan M. Linforth have disagreed with the current

definition of Orphism (as defined in this thesis), positing that the Orphics lacked a

cohesive group, shared no common belief systems and did not have a canon that united

them.[41] In a recent publication, Charles H. Kahn further perpetuates Linforth's sixty-year

old theory that "There is no evidence of a lasting Orphic community of the type founded

by Pythagoras. According to our literary texts, Orphic rites are typically organized by

itinerant priests, like the ones described by Adeimantus in *Republic* II. . ."[42] Kahn

---

[40] Larry J. Alderink, *Creation and Salvation in Ancient Orphism* (Ann Arbor: Scholars Press, 1981) 83.

[41] Ivan M. Linforth, *The Arts of Orpheus* (Berkeley: University of California Press, 1941) 291-292.

[42] Charles H. Kahn, *Pythagoras and the Pythagoreans* (Indianapolis/Cambridge: Hackett Publishing Company, Inc., 2001) 21. This is incorrect, since a number of poems written by Pythagoras were attributed to Orpheus, and were documented by Ion of Chios. The teachings of Orpheus are believed to be older than those of Pythagoras since the former purportedly visited Egypt. This has been referenced in Diogenes Laertius, "Lives of Eminent Philosophers," Trans. R. D. Hicks, (Cambridge Massachusetts: Harvard University Press, 1965) 327.

appears to make no distinction between *Orpheotelestês* who were public in their practice, as opposed to those *Orphikoi* who remained in secret groups. Contrary to these speculations, the entire ritual significance of burying amulets with inscribed formularies served a post-mortem function: to purify the initiate so that he/she could 1) navigate through Hades (A4, B1-B11)[43]; 2) become a hero (B1)[44]; and 3) become divine (i.e., a demi-god; A1-A5, P1-P2, B9).[45] If these actions failed, then the soul would return to the body of a human or animal. Plato's *Phaedo* contains a section wherein Socrates and Cebes discuss the nature, origin and departure of souls to and from Hades. Citing an ancient legend, Socrates shows how the souls of the dead are returned to Earth, that the living obtain their souls from spirits who had already inhabited this Earth. The discussion is broadened even further as Socrates proposes that such souls first inhabit those of plants and animals and should be factored into the origin of souls:

τοῦ σωματοειδοῦς ἀπιθυμιῶ ἀνδεθῖσιν εῆς σῖμα.
Ἐνδοῦνται δή, ὅσπερ εἠκᾶς, εῆς τοιαῦτα ἔθηη
ἀπο→' ὧττ' ἄν καῆ μεμελετηκυῖαι τῖχωσιν ἄν τῖ
β-ῖ.

"And they flit about until through the desire of the corporeal which clings to them they are again imprisoned in a body. And they are likely to be imprisoned in natures which correspond to the practices of their former life."[46]

---

[43] Diogenes Laertius, "Lives of Eminent Philosophers," Trans. R. D. Hicks, (Cambridge Massachusetts: Harvard University Press, 1965) 5. Diogenes claims that those who are initiated into the Orphic mysteries will benefit from their journey to Hades.
[44] Smith, C. and Comparetti, D, "The Petelia Gold Tablet." *The Journal of Hellenic Studies* Vol 3, 1882. 112.
[45] Edmonds, 13-17.

[46] Plato, "*Phaedo*," in: "Euthyphro, Apology, Crito, Phaedo, Phaedrus." Trans. Harold North Fowler. Ed. Jeffrey Henderson. (Cambridge, Massachusetts: Harvard University Press, 2001) 284 and 285, respectively.

The legend of *Er,* in the last book of Plato's *Republic,* best exemplifies the Orphic notion of metempsychosis and the thousand year journey of souls. In it, Er, son of Armenios, a Pamphylian from Asia Minor, dies in battle and returns to his body after seeing the passage of souls from heaven and Earth. The judges of mankind command *Er* to be a messenger, so that he may see that men are once again born into other bodies and animals. It was on this journey that he sees the soul of Orpheus being born into a swan. During this journey to the underworld Er observes:

> ἀπειδΕ διαδικάσειαν, τούς μὰν δικαῆους κελεύ-
> ειν πορεύεσθαι ΤΕν εῆς δεξιαν ΤΕ καῆ ἄνω δια τού
> ούρανού, σημεῆα περιάψαντας τών δεδῆκασμάνων
> ἀν Τᾷ πρᾳθεν, τούς δὰ ἀδίκους ΤΕν εῆς ἀριστεράν
> ΤΕ καῆ κάτω, ἀχοντας καῆ τούτους ἀν Τᾷ απισθεν
> σημεῆα παντων ἀν ἀπραξαν

> "The righteous journey to the right and upwards through the
> heaven with tokens attached to them in front of the judgement passed upon them,
> and the unjust to take the road to the left and downward, they too were wearing
> behind signs of all that had befallen them."[47]

As we shall see in the following chapters, the similarities between the "Orphic" gold lamellae and Plato's account are strikingly similar. In many of these instances, the soul is instructed to turn right (Tablet A4 from Thurri, B1 from Petelia, Italy, and B10 from Hipponion) and to avoid the cypress tree on the left. With respect to Er's account, the Orphic lamellae are more precise in their directions to the deceased, a feature that will be highlighted in the following chapters.

The first literary account of Orpheus that will be of interest to our discussion is that of the <u>Argonautica</u>, written by Apollonius Rhodius in the third century B.C. During

---

[47] Plato, "The Republic: Books VI-X," Trans. Paul Shorey (Cambridge, Massachusetts: Harvard University Press, 2000) 492 and 493, respectively.

the voyage with Jason and nine other heroes, Orpheus calms the drunken Argonauts by

singing a cosmogonic account complete with all the deities of the celestial heavens.[48] His

musical exposition is more than an art form; it works like a magical spell over the men.

The enchanting song cites the rule of Zeus along with the chthonic deities of heaven and

earth, showing the lineage of power as deriving from one source. This preoccupation

with celestial deities, reciting the cosmogonic events that formed the universe, will be an

important feature in the ritual preparation of the gold leaves and papyri that will be

discussed later. The power of Orpheus' magical compositions[49] over living beings as well

as the elements will lend authority to the very texts that were buried with Orphic initiates

in preparation for the afterlife. These texts, it will be shown, are seen as oracles, deriving

from the very poetic, musical prose that flowed from the mouth and lyre of the prophet

from Thrace. Orpheus' power and ability to change events among the living is one aspect

of his influence in the literary and magical tradition. The second feature concerns the

death of the poet and his rebirth, which has Bacchic connotations since Dionysus died

and was reborn. The earliest account lies in a lost play, the _Lycurgia_, by Aeschylus that is

given in the account by Pseudo Eratosthenes in the _Catasterismi_.[50] The _Catasterismi_ or

Katasterismoi is attributed to Eratosthenes of Cyrene (276 B.C. - 194 B.C.), an

astronomer, poet, and director of the library in Alexandria who associates a number of

Greek myths with the creation of constellations. His work recounts the creation of the

---

[48] Apollonius Rhodius, "The Argonautica," Trans. R. C. Seaton (Cambridge, Massachusetts: Harvard University Press, 1967) 37.

[49] Julian, "The Works of the Emperor Julian: Vol. III," Trans. Wilmer Cave Wright (Cambridge, Massachusetts: Harvard University Press, 1953) 237 & 265.

[50] Eratosthenes, "Eratosthenis Catasterismorum Reliquiae : Accedunt Prologomena et Epimetra Tria," Trans. Carolus Robert (Berolini : Apud Weidmannos, 1963) 24.

lyre by Hermes, who gives it to Apollo, who then gives it to Orpheus.[51] Because of

Orpheus' ability to charm animals and humans, Zeus places the lyre in the ninth position

of constellations (of which there are a total of forty-three). Zeus validates the lyre as a

magical instrument capable of delivering oracles, honors Orpheus and the muses, and

essentially validates Orpheus as a prophet-seer. The climax of the story ends with the

Bacchanals or Thracian women, who tear Orpheus to pieces. Orpheus is believed to have

been killed because he betrayed Dionysus for worshipping Apollo and Helios, and for

supposedly hating women because he could not be with Eurydice.[52] Having finally torn

his head from his body, it is thrown into the water and begins to sing hymns to the gods;

Orpheus has triumphed over the powers of metempsychosis and achieves

immortalization according to the power of Zeus. Like Bacchus or Dionysus, the Thracian

poet's head lives on and sings oracles for those who seek it- just as Bacchus' heart is still

beating after the Titans tear him to pieces.[53]

    The following chapters will therefore show that: 1) a belief in metempsychosis of

the soul was a central concern among Orphics; 2) in order for a soul to enter Hades or

---

[51] Euripides, "Select Papyri: Vol. III," Trans. D. L. Page (Cambridge, Massachusetts: Harvard University Press, 1970) 109. In Euripides' *Hypsipyle*, the former queen of Lemnos is taught the lyre by Orpheus while her brother is schooled in Ares' weapons of war.

[52] Anonymous, "Select Papyri: Vol. III," Trans. D. L. Page (Cambridge, Massachusetts: Harvard University Press, 1970) 607. In an anonymous hymn to the Nile, the author claims that in contrast to the ocean and wild animals, women are oblivious to the song of Orpheus. The author cites the lyre as an appropriate instrument for charming such both natural elements and living creatures.

[53] Proclus, "Hymni, Accedunt Hymnorum Fragmenta, Epigrammata, Scholia, Fontium et Locorum Similium Apparatus, Indices," Trans. and Ed. Ernst Vogt. (Wiesbaden, In Kommission bei O. Harrassowitz, 1957) 35, 210, 214.

Heaven, it needed to be purified; 3) the soul is immortal and is caught in the wheel of birth and death; and 4) the ritual and burial practices of using charms, tablets, papyri, and inscriptions serve to help the soul remember its past transgressions (ie., the lake of Mnemosyne = memory = immortality of the soul). Without these formulas, a lamella is rendered useless. The individual must follow the directions in order to become immortal. Mnemosyne is described in terms of this immortality so that the soul remembers his/her sins and can continue past the guardians of the lake. If, on the other hand, the soul disregards these directions and takes a wrong turn, it is led to Lethe or the river of forgetfulness; it is at this point that the soul returns to earth in the form of a man or animal. The belief then, is that these golden tokens are useful as a "map" to the underworld, to be used by the soul. These elements will be discussed further in the following section on these burial finds.

Chapter 3

Material Evidence and Exegesis

Classification of the Leaves

The treating of burial evidence and the interpretation of such material requires

caution by the scholar, as evident from the remains of cults at Eleutherna (Crete) and

Thurii. Both of these cities have revealed numerous lamellae, which will be discussed in

the forthcoming chapters. In an attempt to create a meaningful study of the Orphic gold

lamellae, several scholars, starting with Otto Kern and Gunther Zuntz, have grouped

them into A (Thurii) / B (Eleutherna, Mylopetra, Pharsalos) and / C (Thurii)

classifications (see Appendix 2).[54] Recently, a new addendum to this system has been

proposed by Radcliffe Edmonds, with the Siglum (Abbreviation) P (Pelinna, Thessaly),

Ph (Pherai, Thessaly) and El (Eleutherna) referring to more recent finds.[55] I have

assigned the abbreviation of Sr to represent the uninscribed lamellae[56] (see Appendix 2).

These groupings are based not only on the location of the lamellae (Magna Graecia,

Thessaly or Crete) but on the type of inscriptions, which shall be considered shortly. For

the most up-to-date listing of the published lamellae, please see Appendix 2. Until now,

the shapes of the "leaves" have not been factored into the classification of the groups.

---

[54] O. Kern, *Orphicorum Fragmenta* (Berolini: Apud Weidmannos, 1922). Also: G. Zuntz, *Persephone: Three Essays on Religion and Thought in Magna Graecia* (Oxford: Clarendon Press, 1971).

[55] R. Edmonds, *Roads Not Taken: Explorations of the 'Orphic' Gold Tablets* (Unpublished transcript from the Chicago Humanities Institute, University of Chicago, 1997). p. 19. Received by Prof. Albert Henrichs, spring 2003.

[56] Tzifopoulos, Yannis Z. *The Dionysiac(-Orphic) Lamellae of Crete*: With Contributions on the Archaeological Context by Irene Gavrilaki, Stella Kalogeraki, Eyrydiki Kefalidou, Popi Galanaki and Giorgos Rethemiotakis. (Unpublished manuscript given to me by Professor Yannis Z. Tzifopoulos, University of Crete, 2003) 21-22.

Whereas location, writing, and form of the text provide the necessary elements for classification of the tablets, characteristics of shape have been given little attention. I have compiled the various shapes of the lamellae to fit into the following groups:

1. Ellipsoid, Mouth shape. (Epistomion from Sfakaki, Crete: Fig. 2)[57]
2. Rhombus (Thurii, A1)[58]
3. Oblong (Petelia, B1)[59]
4. Leaves of ivy (Pelinna, P1, P2, 4 B.C.), myrtle, olive[60]
5. Half-moon. (Mylopotamos, 3 B.C.)[61]
6. Rectangular (Eleutherna, E1, 2 B.C. – 1 B.C.)[62]
7. Bone –Shaped (Sfakaki, Crete; uninscribed lamella)
   Sfakaki, Rethymno Museum (Μ[ετάλλινα] 897)[63]

We can surmise that differing shapes among the lamellae served each burial in a unique way. Either the lamella was worn as a protective device (Petelia), placed over the mouth in praise of the afterlife (Sfakaki, Crete), to be held by the initiate or to be placed near the brain for memorization (Thurii). The functionality of an oblong as opposed to an ellipsoid lamella served two different purposes. In order for a metalsmith to fit the Petelia lamella (fourth century B.C.) into the long pentagonal cylinder, it was stamped out in the oblong pattern so that it could be folded over four times (as we shall see later in the

---

[57] Irini Gavrilaki and Yannis Z. Tsifopoulos, "An 'Orphic-Dionysiac' Gold Epistomion from Sfakaki near Rethymno," BCH 122 (1998): 347.

[58] D. Comparetti, "Sibari," *Notizie degli Scavi di Antichita*. Rome: Accademia Nazionale dei Lincei, 3, 1878-1879, 328-331.

[59] Smith, C. and Comparetti, D, "The Petelia Gold Tablet." *The Journal of Hellenic Studies* Vol 3, 1882. 112.

[60] K. Tsantsanoglou., and G. M. Parassoglou, "Two Gold Lamellae from Thessaly," *ΕΛΛΗΝΙΚΑ* 38, 1987, 3-16.

[61] M. Guarducci, "Inscriptiones creticae, Opera et Consilio Friderici Halbherr Collectae.," (Rome: Libreria dello Stato, 1939) 56-60.

[62] A. Joubin, "Inscription Cretoise Relative a l' Orphisme," BCH, 17, 1893, 121-124.

[63] Yannis Z. Tzifopoulos, *The Dionysiac(-Orphic) Lamellae of Crete:* With Contributions on the Archaeological Context by Irene Gavrilaki, Stella Kalogeraki, Eyrydiki Kefalidou, Popi Galanaki and Giorgos Rethemiotakis. (Unpublished manuscript given to me by Professor Yannis Z. Tzifopoulos, University of Crete, 2003). p. 21.

chapter, not all the lamellae were folded like this). The Petelia tablet could have been worn by the individual in daily life, in which case it was placed there during his/her burial. Alternatively, the Petelia necklace could have been prepared specifically for the burial, so that the stamped gold foil could be read in the afterlife. The oblong-shaped Timpone lamellae near Thurii[64] (fourth century B.C.) were quite different, with A1 found close the skeleton's head and A2 – A4 near the right hand. In the bronze hydria from Pharsalos (350-320 B.C.[65]), the rectangular lamella (B2) was found among cremated remains. The only types of lamella (P1, P2) formed into the shape of leaves were those from Pelinna, Thessaly (350-300 B.C.). They were fashioned to resemble individual leaves of ivy, myrtle and olive but actually remind one of the modern symbol of a heart. This form of mimicking plants and vegetation may be influenced by Orpheus' role as the first botanist[66] and the plants that were purportedly used by him for curing illnesses. Perhaps the Orphic metalsmith fashioned lamellae as leaves in order to increase its potency in the afterlife. An oblong or rectangular shape may have been the preferred form of fashioning lamellae since it afforded more space for implementing the required inscriptions. Contrary to these geometrical shapes, a leaf-shaped lamella had space limitations due to its rounded-off edges, resulting in a less uniform arrangement of the magical formulas. In lines 1-6 of P1, the inscription sits horizontally, while line 7 was inscribed vertically (towards the tip of the leaf). In lamella P2, we see the same type of arrangement: lines 1-4 are horizontal, while line 5 was set in vertical fashion. Either there

---

[64] Cavallari, F. S. *Notizie degli Scavi di Antichita*. Rome: Accademia Nazionale dei Lincei, 1879. 316-400.

[65] Verdelis, N.M. Χαλκό τεφροδᾳχος κάλπις ἀκ Φαρσάλων, in Ἀρχ., 1950-1951, pp. 98-105.

[66] Pliny, "Natural History XXIV-XXVII," Trans. W. H. S. Jones (Cambridge, Massachusetts: Harvard University Press, 2001) 145.

was not sufficient room to inscribe the lamella horizontally, or there was some symbolic reason that only the *magoi* could comprehend. A gold epistomion (25 B.C. – A.D. 40) found in Sfakaki Crete, was presumed to "be used as an *epistomion*, lip-band."[67] Either the lip-band had been placed on the mouth before completing the funerary rite, where it fallen subsequent to the decomposition of the body, or it was placed near the base of the head.

Until now we have considered some of the literary and historical conditions that aided in the expression of Orphic eschatology, which now leads us to some of the material evidence that will demonstrate the ritual significance of metempsychosis in this tradition. After completing a discussion of the Olbian bone plates, we shall take into account the burial contexts of the lamellae, their interpretive and ritual functions, while conservatively drawing explanations about the formulaic evidence specific to each lamella.

The Olbia Bone Plates

One of the most significant finds in support of the above aims are the Olbia bone plates from Borysthenes (Olbia), a Scythian province close to the mouth of the Hypanis river (Bug)[68] and near the village of Parutino, dating from the sixth century B.C. The uniqueness of the Olbian bone plates serve as a reminder that not all Dionysian-Orphic evidence can be classified under the heading of gold lamellae. The first part of its history,

---

[67] Irini Gavrilaki and Yannis Z. Tsifopoulos, "An 'Orphic-Dionysiac' Gold Epistomion from Sfakaki near Rethymno," BCH 122 (1998): 346. Along with the Sfakaki lamellae were found three others that were uninscribed. Unfortunately, the publication fails to report the shape of this group.

[68] Herodotus, "*Books III-IV*," Trans. A. D. Godley (Cambridge, Massachusetts: Harvard University Press, 2000) 219.

or the pre-Getic period, is marked by a number of monumental stone structures along

with an agora and temenos dating from 550 B.C. The Olbian people also built a number

of waterway settlements along the Dnieper lagoon and the island of Berezan from 500

B.C. through the sack of the city in the mid first century B.C.[69] A series of finely

polished, rectangular bone plates, averaging five to seven centimeters in length, have

been dated from the sixth century through the Hellenistic period.[70] Excavated by A.N.

Karasev in 1951,[71] they were found in the provincial areas of Olbia and in the temenos of

the agora. Three of these plates now reside in the Institute of Archeology of the

Ukrainian Academy of Sciences (Inventory Number: O-51/3695).[72] Dedications to

Dionysus, Athena, Zeus, and Apollo Delphinios were dated from the fifth century B.C.

The following three bone plates will help us establish this Orphic theory of

metempsychosis, in part due to their fusion of Greek divine names (in full form),

abbreviated sacred words, unintelligible names (*ouces magicae,* or non-Greek names),

symbolic references to rebirth and immortalization, and drawings. For a reproduction of

---

[69] Herodotus. *Book IV.* Trans. R.W. Macan. New York: Arno Press, 1973 36-37. The Olbians are said to have trade relations with the peoples of the Scythian hinterland, who valued the Greek commodities of fishing, metalwork, wine, oil, pottery and textiles. In line 53 of Book IV, Herodotus places the Dniepr (Βορυσθένης) among the three great rivers of the earth (p. 37). Since contact between these two cultures has been documented, there may been some transmission of Orphic beliefs and customs as well.

[70] F. Tinnefeld, "Referat Uber Zwei Russische Aufsatze." *Zeitschrift Fur Papyrologie und Epigraphik* Vol. 38 (1980) 67-71. E. Belin de Ballu, *Olbia; cité antique du littoral nord de la mer Noire* (Leiden, E. J. Brill, 1972) 205. A. Wasowicz, *Olbia Pontique et Son Territoire : L'Aménagement de L'espace* (Paris : Belles-lettres, 1975) 251. M. West, "*The Orphics of Olbia.*" *Zeitschrift Fur Papyrologie und Epigraphik* Vol. 45 (1982) 17.

[71] A.N. Karasev, "Diary of archeological excavations in Olbia in 1951." *In Report of the Olbia expedition for 1951.* (Moscow: Archive of the Institute of Archeology of the Academy of Sciences of the Ukrainian Soviet Socialist Republic, 1951) 47.
[72] A.S. Rusiaeva, "Orfizm I Kul't Dionisa v Ol'vii", *Vestnik Drevney Istorii* Vol. 1 (1978): 87-104.

the bone plates see Figure 3. The following translation illustrates their mythological and

eschatological importance:

(1) β—os ϑάνατos β—os ἀλΕϑεια. Α Διο ορφιϰοι
(2) ΕἠρΕνη πᾳλεμοs ἈλΕϑεια ψευδοs Διο (□)- Α
(3) Διο ἀλΕϑεια - (?) - ψυχΕ - Α   [73]

(1) Life: death: life.-Truth.-A-   -Dio(nysus), Orphic().
(2) Peace: war. Truth: falsehood.-Dio(nysus) □ - A.
(3) Dio(nysus)   -Truth.-(illegible word) . . . soul.-A. [74]

These formulae are of a semiotic nature, in which the symbol or word can be interpreted

on a number of levels. The Olbia bone plates may be seen in a larger context, forming

part of a magical Corpus extrapolated from some Orphic/Bacchic text in the vein of the

Chaldaic Oracles[75] or the *Corpus Hermeticum*. Such a theory is further supported by

Herodotus (4.79) who records that a cult of Bacchos was active during the sixth century

at Olbia.[76] Herodotus also writes of a Thracian tribe, the Getae, who claim to be

immortal.[77] The Getae believe that upon death they do not die but are sent as a messenger

to the god Salmoxis (Zalmoxis) or Gebeleïzis. They also believe, according to Herodotus,

that immortality can be achieved while still living. Eschatologically, 'Life: death' may

denote the Orphic idea of the wheel in which the soul is reborn in another body, a

cyclical relationship that is only ended upon achieving immortality. Truth is opposed to

---

[73] A.S. Rusiaeva, 87-88.
[74] West 17.

[75] Julian, "The Works of the Emperor Julian: Vol. I," Trans. Wilmer Cave Wright (Cambridge, Massachusetts: Harvard University Press, 1962) 483. The secret teachings of the Chaldeans celebrated astrology and worshipped Helios or the god of the Seven Rays.
[76] Herodotus. *Book IV*. Trans. R.W. Macan: 53-55.
[77] Herodotus, "Books III-IV," Trans. A. D. Godley (Cambridge, Massachusetts: Harvard University Press, 2000) 295-299.

falsehood, and they are juxtaposed in the plates 1 & 2 by the letters "A," "□," and an illegible word.[78] The significance of such a mystical language can be explained, in part, by the writings of the Neoplatonists who flourished in the third century A.D. One of the most influential of the Neoplatanists was the philosopher and scholar Porphyry (234–305 A.D.) who wrote works on metaphysics and paganism. Iamblichus (245-325 A.D. most likely studied under Porphyry in Rome, writing on the rites and theologies of the Orphics, Persians, Egyptians, and Chaldaeans (see the reference to "Sacred Nations" referred to below). Since Porphyry and Iamblichus wrote commentaries on the subject of Orphism, including the mystical practices of this tradition, it may perhaps shed some light on the Olbian bone plates. An important Neo-Platonic distinction between the use of Greek and non-Greek words in mystical language is found in Porphyry's cynical questions to his student Iamblichus of Chalcis (242-3 AD). Porphyry asks why sorcerers must use "meaningless and foreign words" in ritual, in which Iamblichus replies:

> Barbarous names maybe unintelligible to us, but they are meaningful at the Divine level. The precise terms used do count, because they are not formed by conventional agreement but actually resemble Divine realities. The languages of Sacred Nations is (sic) to be preferred because they preserve ancient and hallowed forms inviolate, whereas Greek is spoiled through innovation.[79]

A jagged or zig-zag symbol (   ) appears on plates 1 & 2 and may signify a thunderbolt, possibly that of Zeus who is the father of Dionysus, and in certain

---

[78] A.S. Rusiaeva, 89.

[79] Iamblichus of Chalcis, *De Mysteriis Aegyptiorum,* ed. Stephen Ronan, trans. Thomas Taylor & Alexander Wilder (Hastings, E. Sussex, England: Chthonios Books: 1989) 7. Here, Iamblichus argues for a multi-dimensional theory of symbolic language, with respect to divine invocation. While Porphyry shows the importance of ideas behind a conventional language (somewhat imitating Hermogenes's argument), Iamblichus maintains the opposite; This particular argument bears striking similarity with Plato's *Cratylus,* in which language is either conventional (*nomos*) or based on "true" forms of nature (*physis*) given by the gods.

cosmogonies brings the universe to its totality after castrating Kronos/Chronos.[80] These

symbols may also refer to a serpent, the form taken by Zeus as he mates with

Persephone. The zig-zag can be seen as passwords to be uttered by the initiate, having

been found in tablets B11 (Sicily) and Ph (Pherai, Thessaly). Whether or not this symbol

is indeed Zeus's thunderbolt is left for speculation; the insertion of this symbol, on the

other hand, would not be out of place since it was Zeus's thunderbolt which destroyed

the Titans (consistent with references to thunder and lightning in lamellae A1-A3). It was

the soot of this ash from the Titans that created man, who was thought to have a titanic

nature of good and bad.[81] Man's sin is believed to derive from the wrong doings of the

Titans who killed the beloved king Dionysus. The same kind of zig-zag symbol, although

varied, is found on the reverse side of the second tablet, which M.L. West interprets as

IAX or *Iacchus*. [82] Interestingly, Iacchus is an Athenian and Thracian name for Dionysos,

with similar etymologies ranging from Eiraphiotes to Euios, and Eleuthereus.[83] The

abbreviation or collapsing of sacred Greek names (*Logoi Theologoumenoi*) like *IAX* may

have been one of convenience since the full names were known to the initiates, and were

consequently made to be a secret invocation among the *Bacchoi* of Olbia. Anaximander

---

[80] The Derveni Theology recounts the overthrow of Kronos (the Sun, "*aidoia*", translated as Genitals) by his son Zeus (Laks and Most, p. 14-15; PDERV, Col. XIII). Previous to this encounter Kronos castrates his father Ouranos and assumes power (Col. XIV, p. 15), a violent fate that he himself will ultimately be dealt at the hands of his own son.
[81] Xenocrates, *Frammenti / Senocrate, Ermodoro*, ed. and trans. by Margherita Isnardi Parente. (Napoli : Bibliopolis, 1982) 239.

[82] West 17. During the procession of the initiates in the *Mysteria* festival from Athens to Eleusis, chants of "*Iakch' o Iakche*" were common among the participants. Burkert, Walter. *Greek Religion*, (Cambridge, Massachusetts: Harvard University Press, 1998) 287-288.

[83] K. Kerényi. *Dionysos : Urbild des unzerstörbaren Lebens* (Munich: Langen Mueller, 1976) 405.

of Miletus tells of Pythagorean initiates who memorized various oral teachings (*sumbola,* translated as 'passwords or tokens') known as the *acusmata*; this rite had particular social significance in the order, as a rite of passage, and to ensure that the initiate would be recognized by the gods as an adept in the afterlife. [84] To the left of this *IAX* inscription we find a rectangular model divided into seven areas, each containing a circular pattern within it. Looking toward the Pythagorean and Neo-Platonic traditions, the references to the number seven are quite significant.[85] The myth, as preserved in the hymns of the Eudemian Theogonies (ca. 400 B.C), and Rhapsodies (100 B.C.),[86] tell of the Titans luring the infant Dionysos and cutting him up into seven pieces. They then proceeded to cook and taste him before they are killed by Zeus' thunderbolt. Athena takes the heart of the child-king and so he is born again.[87] The reverse side on the third tablet from Olbia (4.8 x 3.5 x 0.5 cm) has an interesting design that is abstract and difficult to decipher, its purpose apparently to obscure the true meaning of the message so that only insiders of

---

[84] G.S. Kirk, J.E. Raven, and M. Schofield, *The Presocratic Philosophers: Second Edition* (Cambridge: Cambridge University Press, 1983) 229-230.

[85] Philolaus of Croton (470 B.C. to 385 B.C.) in: Diels, H. and W. Kranz, *Die Fragmente der Vorsokratiker* (in three volumes), 6th edition, (Dublin and Zürich: Weidmann, 1952) 421-439. Huffman, C. A., *Philolaus of Croton: Pythagorean and Presocratic*, (Cambridge: Cambridge University Press, 1993) 54-77 and 202-215. Up until the fifth and fourth centuries B.C., the lyre had seven strings, which has its place in the harmonic intervals of "cosmic music" as proposed by the Pythagoreans Archytas and Philolaus, and confirmed by Plato and Aristotle.

[86] Kern, O. *Orphicorum Fragmenta.* (Berolini: Apud Weidmannos, 1922) 147 and 173.

[87] Clement of Alexandria, "*Exhortation to the Greeks and The Rich Man's Salvation to the Newly Baptized*" Trans. G.W. Butterworth. Ed. G.P. Goold. (Cambridge, Massachusetts: Harvard University Press, 1999) 38-39.

the mystery cult could decipher its meaning and function.[88] The Olbia bone plates

therefore share a common system of beliefs with the Orphic gold lamellae in the

following manner:

1. Adherence to and respect for Dionysus (Διο / Διο (□)).
2. Recognition of Orpheus as part of this belief system (ορφικοι).
3. Life (β‒oς) is a cycle, it ends not in death, but through revelation of truth / knowledge / gnosis (άλEϑεια).
4. Use of passwords or *sumbola* and the recognition of magical symbols (□ - A). Belief in the soul.

As we shall see in the following analysis of the lamellae, the path to

immortality was experienced and achieved through king Dionysus. The evidence

from Olbia shows the extent to which a theory of reincarnation existed during the

fifth century B.C. One may view the reference to "truth" and the symbols contained

throughout as keys to the afterlife, ritual formulas that were necessary for the soul to

achieve redemption, purity, and acceptance among other *magoi*. We now turn to the

evidence (where documented) regarding the gold lamellae.

Burial Finds

The texts on the gold sheets we shall now discuss were primarily written in

hexameter verse, the crude letters being scratched on the surface, with the sheets then

folded and having creases in them, which has led to further difficulties in translation.

Some of the tablets have been found near the head of the skeleton (Timpone Grande,

Thurii, The National Archaeological Museum of Naples, Inv # 111463, 111464) while

others were placed near the hand (Timpone Piccolo, National Archaeological Museum of

---

[88] A.S. Rusiaeva, "Orfizm I Kul't Dionisa v Ol'vii", *Vestnik Drevney Istorii* Vol. 1 (1978): 89.

Naples, Inv # 111625, 111623, 111624). In these specific cases, I shall note, when available, the specific location of the gold plates.

The fourth century B.C. plates from Thurii, South Italy, now in the National Museum at Naples, illustrate the importance of ritual formulary. Like most of the gold plates, the first hexameter begins with an introduction "I come; I am; Out of the pure I come," and in some instances a third party speaks on behalf of the initiate who is passing on to the afterlife. In tablet A1 from Thurii (Nat. Mus. Naples, Inv. 111625), the initiate addresses a divine entity, as if seeking entrance to the heavens:

Ἔρχομαι ἦκ κοθαρ᾽,<ν> κοθρά, χθον–<ων> βασ–λεια
Ε᾽κλός Ε᾽βο<υ>λε᾽ς τε καὴ ὠθάνατοι θεοὴ ὢλλοι
καὴ γῶρ ἀγ᾽ν ἠμ᾽ν γῆνος ἄλβιον ε᾽χομαι ε᾽μεν.
ἀλ<λ> ά με Μο<→>ρ᾽{α} ἀδάμασ<σ>ε {καὴ ἁθάνατοι θεοὴ ὢλλοι} καὴ
ὡσ{σ}τεροβλότα κεραυνῒι.
κη κλο<υ> δ᾽ ἠξῆπταν βαρυπενθέος ἀργαλέοιο,
ἁμερτο<υ᾽>> δ᾽ ἐπέβαν στεφάνο<υ> ποσὴ καρπαλᾶμοισι,
δεσ<σ>ποάνας δ᾽<ε> ῾πὰ κὰλπον ηδυν χθον–ας βασιλε–ας·
{ιμερτοδαπὴβανστεμανουποσικαρπασιμοισι}
῾ἄλβια καὴ μακαριστέ, θε᾽ς δ᾽ ησηι ὢντι βροτο→ο᾽.
ὑριφος ἦς γάλ᾽ ηπετον[89]

Pure I come from the pure, Queen of those below,
and Eukles and Eubuleus, and the other immortal gods;
For I boast that I am of your blessed race.
But fate has mastered me and the Thunderer, striking with his lightning.
I flew out of the circle of wearying heavy grief;
I came on with swift feet to the desired crown;
I passed beneath the bosom of the Mistress, Queen of the Underworld,
I came out with swift feet from the desired crown.
"Blessed and enviable one, a god you shall be instead of mortal."
A kid I fell into milk.[90]

---

[89] A. Bernabe and A.I. Jimenez San Cristobal. *Instrucciones Para El Mas Alla: Las Laminillas Orficas de Oro*. (Madrid: Ediciones Clasicas, 2001) 270.

[90] Edmonds, 13.

The initiate is addressing Persephone, the queen of the underworld, who was abducted by Hades. It was custom for magical formulary, Babylonian[91] and Egyptian papyri/tablets, and Orphic texts to invoke (*Peithein Theous*) a god/goddess in order to procure some outcome. In many instances, as in the Timpone Grande Tablet (A4), the divine personages are not readily identifiable; the arcane nature of such a formulary or "formula" is meant to be evasive, so that only the *magus* can utilize them. Some of the more obscure Orphic divinities are addressed as 'Stayers, All-Accomplishers, Well-named Daemon, Master, Healer, All-Subduer, Sickle-Bearer."[92] In other respects, Persephone holds particular favor in the Orphic tradition since she can act as a mediator between the souls and Hades, who is her consort. Interestingly, in the Thurii plates, the writer does not pay homage to the primal forces of night and chaos (or some of the Chthonic deities like Ge or Oceanus) but to Persephone. In the Rhapsodic theogony, Zeus mates with his mother Rhea-Demeter, who both take the shape of serpents. Rhea-Demeter then gives birth to Persephone-Kore and subsequently abandons her daughter. Metamorphosing into serpent form once again, Zeus mates with Persephone-Kore in

---

[91] *Babylonian Magic and Sorcery: Being The Prayers of the Lifting of the Hand* Trans. and Ed. Leonard W. King. (London: Luzac and Co., 1896) 26-27. The Sumerian cuneiform texts and incantations, ceremomies, and prayers from the 76 cuneiform tablets in the excavation of Nineavah (British Museum, Inv. # not published) refer to this underworld queen as *Damkina / IR.NI.NA /* queen of the abyss and of the gods, wife of *Ia* (king of the abyss), who has a dual nature like that of Persephone-Demeter. Her invocation is hoped to cure those diseases brought on by an eclipse of the Moon. *Damkina*'s inclusion in these tablets accompany an incantation to *Marduk*, similar to the Orphic need to invoke a variety of gods for fear of retribution.

[92] Harrison, <u>Prolegomena</u> 666. I quote Harrison because no other translations of these names have been attempted. In such cases of obscurity, one may propose that *Peithein Theous* were apparently written so that only the magus or high priest could understand them. They may refer to one deity who has many names or a number of "guardians" who decide the entrance of souls. In any case, we see a mixture of these forms within the gold tablets, with no apparent adherence to rules or protocol regarding their application.

Crete, producing the child Dionysos.[93] Once again, we see the multiplicity of meanings

from the names "Eukles and Eubuleus," titles found in both the Orphic and Eleusinian

hymns: Eukles has been found in connection with Hades/Pluto, and conjointly Eukles

and Eubuleus are names for Zeus, Zagreus, Phanes, and Hades-Plouton, ie. the

"subterranean Zeus." Considering the emphasis placed on cosmogony and the entire

pantheon of entities worshipped among Orphics, the recognition of "other Gods and

Daemons" would be appropriate since no initiate would want to offend the Gods. Also

prevalent in the Orphic texts, which we see in the Thurii plates, is a confession that the

initiate has paid the penalty for unrighteous deeds, alluding to the death of Dionysos (A1-

A4, P1-P2, and Ph). The Titans, although not completely devouring the child Dionysos,

consumed a part of him and thus absorbed his essence. When Zeus killed the Titans with

his thunderbolt (cited in the Thurii text), their dust led to the birth of humans. It is from

this myth that we begin to understand the "Titanic" nature of humans: blessed by the

divinity of Dionysos and cursed by the evil nature of the Titans who sought destruction

of the God-King Bacchus.

The Soul's Journey

The Orphic, then, is instructed to write down a password that allows him/her to

gain entrance into a world where only purified souls are allowed entry (B1, B10, B11).

Birth, death, and rebirth take place in the wheel of life, a circular event independent of

---

[93] Clement of Alexandria, *"Exhortation to the Greeks and The Rich Man's Salvation to the Newly Baptized"* Trans. G.W. Butterworth. Ed. G.P. Goold. (Cambridge, Massachusetts: Harvard University Press, 1999) 35-37.

time and dependent on the soul's actions during mortal life. In the discussion between

Socrates and Phaedrus, souls must journey thousands of years before they can take

corporeal form:

εἰς μὰν γὼρ τ᾿ α᾿τ᾿ ἄθεν ἔκει
Ε ψυχὲ ἐκῶστη ο᾿κ ῶφικνε→ται ἠτ᾿ν μυρ—ων· ο᾿
γῶρ πτερο᾿ται πρ᾿ τοσο᾿του χρᾳνου,

"For each soul returns to the place whence it came in ten thousand years;
for it does not regain its wings before that time has elapsed."[94]

The Rhapsodic Theogony (200-100 B.C.)[95] makes no distinction between animal,

plant, or human. A soul is considered immortal, passing through any number of animal

and human bodies. The Rhapsodies outline how many years it will take for the soul to

cycle back to the beginning: nine thousand years for the god who bears false testimony

versus three hundred years for purified souls.[96] Furthermore, the Thurii initiate (A1)

acknowledges having escaped the "sorrowful, weary circle into the diadem desired."[97]

Returning to the diadem, a cloth headband or crown, may refer to Dionysus who was to

be crowned king by Zeus. The initiate knows, and is able to execute through lucid

imagery, where he has been and the desired destination for his soul. Rebirth is further

facilitated by the initiate's willingness to sink "beneath the bosom of the Mistress,"

another reference to Persephone, who herself returns to Hades six months out of the year.

The use of allegory in the Orphic gold lamellae allows the adept to incorporate the

---

[94] Plato, "Phaedrus," in: "Euthyphro, Apology, Crito, Phaedo, Phaedrus." Trans. Harold North Fowler. Ed. Jeffrey Henderson. (Cambridge, Massachusetts: Harvard University Press, 2001) 480 and 481, respectively.

[95] Kern, O. *Orphicorum Fragmenta.* (Berolini: Apud Weidmannos, 1922) 147 and 173.

[96] Kern, O. *Orphicorum Fragmenta.* (Berolini: Apud Weidmannos, 1922) 295 and 231.

[97] Edmonds, 13.

concept of metempsychosis within a whole range of mythical stories from that of

Persephone to that of Dionysus.

The Tablet of Caecilia Secundina (A5), although of later date (circa first to

second century A.D.), bears striking similarity to the Thurii remains. Written on a thin,

gold foil, it measures 75 mm x 2mm in size, having been found in Rome near the Ostia

tombs, it now resides in the British Museum (Inventory # 3154). The translation is as

follows:

> Ἔρχεται ἡκ καθαρ᾽ν καθαρῷ, χθον‑ων βασ‑λεια,
> Ἐ᾽κλεες Ἐ᾽βουλε□ τε Δι᾽ς τήκος· ζλλῷ δήχεσθεε
> Μνημοσ|᾽νης τᾶδε δ᾽ρον ῷο‑διμον ῷνθρόποισιν.
> Ἰαικιλ‑α Σεκουνδε‑να νᾶμωι ἐθι δ‑α γεγ᾽σα.'[98]
>
> Pure she comes from the pure, Queen of those below the earth,
> Eukles and Eubouleus, child of Zeus, radiant one. I have
> this gift of memory, famed in song among men.
> Caecilia Secundina, come, having become a goddess by the custom.[99]

Here the intermediary, or quite possibly an Orphic priest, (*Orpheotelestae, Agyrtai,*

Chrêsmôdiai[100]) may have consulted with Caecilia Secundina in creating this amulet so

she could "redeem" her soul, a common practice elaborated on by Plato in the *Republic*

(see Chapter II). The curious question still remains: who was responsible for the

production and incision of these gold plates? Were they part of the *Orpheotelestae*'s

---

[98] D. Comparetti, "Laminetta Orfica di Cecilia Secundina," *Atene e Roma* 54-55 (1903): 161.

[99] Edmonds, 14.

[100] The distinction is made among priests trained by Orpheus (*teletai*), those taught by Musaios and the ῷκροατα‑ (translated as followers) who simply listen to Orphic poems. For more, see Joseph Fontenrose, *The Delphic Oracle: Its Responses and Operations* (Berkeley: University of California Press, 1978) 162.

craft, selling magical formulary to people who were about to die? Or were they contracted out to metalsmiths who specialized in working these precious metals? Consider the following two-fold process: in this case, Caecilia may have hired an Orphic priest who was to prepare the magical verses to be inscribed in gold by a metalsmith. Whoever was responsible for the actual content would have had knowledge of the Orphic tradition as we see in the Caecilia tablet. The exact authorship of these lamellae are extremely difficult to trace, since the author did not inscribe their name or give any hint as to their affiliation or city of birth. Where possible, we shall return to this topic of authorship in the gold lamellae. Caecilia is portrayed as one of the pure ones, of pure origin. The reference to the "Pure Queen" must surely be Persephone, who resides in Hades and mediates the affairs of the deceased. As in the Thurii context, Eukles and Eubouleus[101] are again invoked, either as an invocation to Hades and Zeus or to Dionysos or Zagreus, who is the "Child of Zeus."

In our analysis of the Caecilia Secundina tablet, we encounter a new allegorical use of memory. Although this term, conceptually speaking, is not new to the Orphic views on eschatology, the use of the word "Μνημοσ | ´νης"[102] or "armour" (A5,3) is rare in the context of memory. References to the soul's memorization in the lamellae refer either to water (Plato uses the word *Anamnesis* as the same meaning) or the lake of memory (Mnemosyne) which the soul must drink of to obtain immortality. The "armour"

---

[101] Clement of Alexandria, "*Exhortation to the Greeks and The Rich Man's Salvation to the Newly Baptized*" Trans. G.W. Butterworth. Ed. G.P. Goold. (Cambridge, Massachusetts: Harvard University Press, 1999) 29. In his discussion of Dionysus and Demeter, Clement mentions Eubouleus as one of the aborigines who inhabited Eleusis and who was a hierophant at Athens. Since he is discussing these "clans" in terms of Demeter and Dionysus, we can only infer that this priesthood pledged allegiance to these gods.
[102] Edmonds, 4.

of memory here is allegorical, possibly referring to the protection of the soul from forgetfulness; the suppliant must remember past transgressions in order to become a god, for it is purity of mind that is continually emphasized among the Orphic tablets. The invocation calls for the child of Zeus, Zagreus/Dionysos either to receive the armour or bestow it upon the mendicant as a key of entry, a final rite that ensures Caecilia Secundina's place among the gods as a daemon. The sequences of ritual formularies in Orphic tablets appear to be constructed in such a logical fashion: the soul is addressed within the divine lineage, followed by some reference to memory, and concluding with a confirmation of salvation for the suppliant. In attributing various Orphic ideas to the philosophy of Heraclitus, Clement in the *Stromateis* claims: "Orpheus wrote:

ψυχόσά γῶρ θῶνατος ᾿δωρ γενέσθαι, ᾿δατι
δῆ θῶνατος γόν γενέσθαι· έκ γός,δά ᾿δωρ
γ—νεται, ῆξ ᾿δατος δά ψυξη

As souls change into water
on their way through death,
so water changes into earth.
And as water springs from earth,
So from water does the soul.[103]

It is not necessary to quote the subsequent lines since no evidence points to Orphic ideas in Heraclitus's writings.[104] Whether Clement is referring to the cycle of rebirth or a material argument in which opposites are returned to their former state is not certain. Attributing quotations to Orpheus was common among ancient writers, who either paraphrased statements or took bits and pieces to their liking. The authors of the gold

---

[103] Heraclitus, *Fragments*. Trans. Brooks Haxton. (London: Penguin Classics, 2001) 42. fr. 68.

[104] For more on Orphism and Heraclitus see G.S. Kirk, *Heraclitus: The Cosmic Fragments* (Cambridge: University Press, 1970) 339.

tablets, I believe, were not attempting to re-create a symbolic language reflecting the salvation of the soul. Ritual formulary also had the function and/or symbolic nature of separating material reality from the divine or true state of nature, creating, in a sense, a super-reality to prepare initiates for immortality (i.e. the Orphic soul looks to return to its immortal parents, Zeus, Persephone, earth and starry heaven, etc). Orphism was not considered a "common" religious practice among the Athenian or the Italic peoples, for it dealt with *arcana* and rites that were dependent on secret and unspeakable names (*apokryphōi*), allegorical symbols (*krypta*) that were accessible only to those trained as *Bacchoi* or *Teletai*.

Topography and Landscape

Another possible reference to "memory" can be found in the Timpone Grande Tablet (A4). This rectangular gold slip was excavated in a large tomb in the commune of Corigliano-Calabro in South Italy and now resides in the National Museum of Naples (Inventory # 111463). A number of vertical and horizontal lines, caused by initial folding and crumpling of the tablet, complicated the initial translations, proving it difficult to ascertain the exact text. The translation by R. Edmonds reads as follows:

Ἀλλ' ἀπᾶταν ψυχὲ προλ–πηι φῶος ὦελ–οιο,
δεξι˙ν Ε.ΘΙΑΣ δ' ἠξι. <έ>ναι πεφυλαγμήνον ε μζλα πζντα·
χα→ρε παθ˙ν τ˙ πζθημα τ˙ δ' ο˙πω πρᾶσθ' {ε} ἠπεπᾶνθεις·
θε˙ς ἡγένου ἠξ ὦνθρῖπου· ὑριφος ἠς γῶλα ὑπετες.
χα→ρ<ε> χα→ρε· δεξιῶν ἀδοιπᾶρ<εή>
λειμ˙νζς θ' {ε} ἀεροίς καὴ ὦλσεα Φερσεφονε–ας.[105]

But when the soul leaves the light of the sun,

---

[105] D. Comparetti, "Sibari," *Notizie degli Scavi* 3 (1879): 156.

go straight to the right, having kept watch on all things very well.
Hail, you having experienced the experience. This you had not experienced
before. A gold you have become from a man. A kid you fell into milk.
Hail, Hail; making your way to the right,
The sacred meadows and groves of Phersephoneia.[106]

The journey of the soul begins with a departure from the sun (helios), a common reference to Zeus who watches over the world of men. While exact meaning of Ennoia (Ε.ΘΙΑΣ; ΕΙΟΑΣ ; ΕΝΟΙΑΣ ; ΣΝΝΟΙΑΣ) in line 2 is not known, it may represent the spring Lethe to which the soul must avoid drinking (similar to springs in tablets B2-B11). In tablets B2-B11, the soul is told to avoid drinking the spring near a glowing white cypress tree on the right. Instead, the individual is urged to walk toward the lake of memory or Mnemosyne. Other explanations for line 2 of the Timpone Grande might include "To the right you shall find the spring of Ennoia" or "To the right you shall find a spring near the cypress tree Ennoia." What if Ε.ΘΙΑΣ were another epithet for Hades or the groves of Persephone? Ennoia is a unique reference, and does not show itself in any of the other gold plates that refer to the sacred lake. Ε.ΘΙΑΣ, therefore, is purposefully positioned in the beginning of the A4 inscription in order to keep the initiate's concentration focused. The soul must be careful in his/her journey throughout this underworld landscape, taking heed not to be distracted by curious things like Ε.ΘΙΑΣ, a glowing white cypress tree, or Lethe. As in B2-B11, A4 may reference memory in order to help the soul navigate through this complex and bewildering topography. Directing the soul to the right has other parallels, as in the Petelia tablet (south Italy), where the

---

[106] Edmonds, 14.

soul is not to drink of the "well-spring" near the House of Hades but from the "Lake of Memory." Well-springs near Hades are often referred to as Lethe, the lake of Forgetfulness. Drinking of this water would inevitably plunge the soul back into another human or animal body, perpetuating the wheel of life and of consciousness *ad infinitum.*[107] As if temptation would be a factor, the soul is cautioned against drinking from this lake by some outside entity/mediator. Three tablets from Eleuthernae, Crete (L. 55mm x 7mm; 62 mm x 8mm; 56mm x 10mm, respectively) cite "The ever-flowing spring on the Right, by the Cypress."[108]

Metempsychosis, as we have seen, depended on the purification and memory of the soul, a particularly Orphic belief. These beliefs have been expounded through the gold tablets, which have a ritual function for the deceased *Orphikoi.* Even as we consider the use, function and exegesis of these tablets in the "mystery cults," these beliefs were taken up by other philosophers such as Plato. In Book X of Plato's *Republic*, Lethe is described in terms of the River of Neglectfulness, so that any man who drank more than his share would forget everything. Conversely, Mnemosyne is equated with the River of Memory, the water that purifies the soul and makes men immortal, whereby the other souls are:

ἑσπάρας γιγνομένης παρά τὰν ᾿Αμέλητα ποταμὰν

---

[107] C. Watkins, "Orphic Gold Leaves and the Great Way of the Soul: Strophic Style, Funerary Ritual Formula, and Eschatology in *How to Kill a Dragon* (Oxford: Oxford University Press, 1995) 283-284.

[108] Edmonds, 15-16.

"Camped at eventide by the River of Forgetfulness."[109]

The reference by Socrates, "and keep our soul unspotted from the world"

(νομίζοντες ἀθάνατον ψυχὲν καὴ δυνατὲν πάντα μὰν κακα ἀνέχεσθαι)[110] is

a probable reference to the Titanic myth in which man inherits the evil nature of the

Titans.[111] In considering the transmission of knowledge, and the transformation of

conscious states from this life to the next, the influence of Orphic eschatology on

Plotinus is clearly evident: "With respect to memory, it must be considered whether souls

on departing from these places recollect (what happened to them on the Earth) or whether

this is the case with some souls, but not with others; and likewise, whether they have a

recollection of all things, or of certain things only."[112] Plotinus not only confirms the

Orphic ritual use of memory in the afterlife, but more importantly, alludes to a theory of

metempsychosis. Although Plotinus makes the distinction between events that happened

on Earth and elsewhere, the latter statement shows otherwise; is Plotinus referring to

earthly memories or to memories of past lives that the soul has no recollection of? Let us

now look at some other lamellae that warn the soul of the impending dangers that it may

encounter before reaching immortalization.

---

[109] Plato, "The Republic: Books VI-X," Trans. Paul Shorey (Cambridge, Massachusetts: Harvard University Press, 2000) 516 and 517, respectively.

[110] Plato, "The Republic: Books VI-X," Trans. Paul Shorey. 518 and 519, respectively.

[111] Plato, "The Republic: Book X," *Great Dialogues of Plato* (New York: Mentor, 1984) 422.

[112] Plotinus, *Select Works of Plotinus,* Ed. G.R.S. Meade, Trans. Thomas Taylor (London: G. Bell and Sons, Ltd., 1941) 241.

Not all of the inscriptions are so uniform in the approach to describing or directing

the soul through this mystical landscape. In some respects, the soul is challenged by

questions, therefore being required to provide the appropriate answer (A5, B1-B11). As

stated above, the Lake of Memory is not always found on the right; other inscriptions

direct the soul in the opposite direction. In the bronze *hydria* (Museum of Volos,

Inventory # X 18775) found at Pharsalos, dating from the fourth century B.C., a gold

tablet (B2, Museum of Volos, Inv. # M 65) was found inside with the following

inscription:

Ε η ρ η σεις 'Αάδαο δάμοις ἠνδήξια κρὖνην,
πῶρ δ' αˮτόι λευκὲν ἐστηκυ⁻αν κυπῶρισσον·
ταˮτης τός κρὖνης μηδά σχεδάθεν πελῶσηισθα·
πράσσω δ' εˮρῦσεις τ˙ Μνημοσˮνης ῷπ˙ λ⁻μνης
ψυχρˮν ˙δωρ προ<ρέον>· φˮλακες δ' ἠπˮπερθεν ηασιν·
οῆ δὲ σ<ε> ε⁻ρῦσονται ἅ τι χρέος ε⁻σαφικῶνεις·
το⁻ς δά σί ε μῶλα πῶσαν ῷληθε⁻ην καταλῆξαι·
ε⁻πε⁻ν· Γός πα⁻ς ε⁻μι καὴ Οˮρανο⎕ ῷστ<ερᾳεντος>·
'Αστήριος ἄνομα· δίψηι δ' ε⁻μ' α˚ος· ῷλλῶ δᾷτε μοι πιήν· ῷπ˙
τός κρὖνης'.[113]

'In the halls of Hades you will find on the right a spring with a white cypress
standing beside it. Go nowhere near this spring, but farther on you will find cold
water running from the lake of Memory. Above it are guards who will ask you
what you want. You tell them the whole truth, and say 'I am a child of Earth and
starry Heaven; my name is Asterios. I am dry with thirst; allow me to drink from
the spring'.[114]

Previous excavations noted in this discussion have been limited to those of skeletal

remains with which the gold "leaves" were found. Not so in this case; here we see a

cremation burial that utilizes Orphic ritual, placing the remains with a prescription for the

[113] Verdelis, N.M. Χαλκό τεφροδᾳχος κάλπις ἀκ Φαρσάλων, in 'Αρχ., (1950-
1951) 97.

[114] Donna C. Kurtz., and John Boardman, *Greek Burial Customs* (London: Thames and
Hudson, 1971) 210.

afterlife. The formula has even been customized for the individual, citing the name

"Asterios" in ritualistic fashion. Asterios could possibly be the person whose ashes lie in

the *hydria* and commissioned the gold leaves. Imagery such as the white cypress,[115]

shown in the previous examples, has allegorical parallels in the primitive fertility rites

relating to the Tree of Life and the birth of Adonis. Asterios must proclaim to be a child

of the chthonic elements of "Earth and Starry Heaven," to either 1) claim divinity and/or

2) to not offend these gods.

The symbolic nature of these gold leaves ensured the soul its salvation through

the afterlife. As stated in my hypothesis, the text is a material manifestation of Orphic

theology, its written contents meant to guide the soul in the afterlife. The references in

Plato, Pindar and others have adequately demonstrated the parallels to Orphic

eschatology and its need to express itself up until the death of the initiate. Ritual

inscription and the tradition of writing formularies served: 1) a material function among

the social circles of these "cults," so that formulas could and hymns could be shared

among Orphics; 2) a tradition for handing down knowledge among *teletai*, 3) encoding

arcana/krypta/Gnōsis, and 4) as a ritual tradition, complete with rules, standards of

invocation, and a belief in a divine language that *teletai* could interpret and utilize in

achieving apotheosis. Consequently, only a strong belief in metempsychosis and an

---

[115] In looking to eastern parallels, a series of cuneiform texts from Babylonia and Assyria contain directions in which plants and woods, namely the cypress tree '*šurmînu / šurmîni* are to be used in the ritual invocation of gods. The anointing of *urmînu*-oil served in the supplication of the male deity in the form of a star named *Sibziana* and *Ishtar*, the "lady of heaven and Earth, the splendour of the four quarters, the first-born of sin." Leonard W. King, *Babylonian Magic and Sorcery: Being The Prayers of the Lifting of the Hand* (London: Luzac and Co., 1896) 6, 115-116. While other plants, herbs and vegetation are used in these initial offerings, the *urmînu*-oil appears to be of special significance.

adherence to such a system could lead to a glorification of writing that had implications beyond the material realm and into the other "spheres," whether they be Hades or those mentioned by the Neo-Platonists. The Egyptians utilized both material objects and hieroglyphic texts in their burial customs, believing that they would help the Pharaoh and others in his journey. In this sense, the Greek and south Italian mystery cults showed the same respect for immortality and the transmission of writing as a mystical thing to be used beyond the mortal realm. Writing formulary inscriptions had to be something concrete, material, enduring, and immutable for it to have been of use in a non-material realm such as Hades. The implications here are numerous and leave us with more questions. Orphic eschatology is complex, since it holds that something as material as writing can transcend this world and make an imprint on the *psyche* of the soul, creating a virtual road map to immortality.

Chapter 4

Gold Tablets

A Unified System?

In the previous chapter, the classificatory system of Kern, Zuntz and Edmonds were briefly highlighted. In an effort to classify the Orphic gold lamellae, several scholars, starting with Otto Kern and Gunther Zuntz, have grouped them into A (Thurii) / B (Eleutherna, Mylopetra, Pharsalos) and / C (Thurii) classifications (see Appendix 2).[116] Recently, a new addendum to this system has been proposed by Radcliffe Edmonds, with the Siglum (Abbreviation) P (Pelinna, Thessaly), Ph (Pherai, Thessaly) and El (Eleutherna) referring to more recent finds.[117] I have assigned the abbreviation of Sr to represent the uninscribed lamellae[118] (see Appendix 2). These classifications are based not only on the location of the lamellae (Magna Graecia, Thessaly or Crete) but on the type of inscriptions which shall be looked at shortly. Henceforth, (B2, 17) will signify the classification (group) of the tablet followed by the line number. Groups A & B (4th B.C.-2nd B.C.) from Thurii, Rome (A1-A4); Pelinna, Thessaly (P1, P2); Petelia, Italy (B1); Pharsalos, Thessaly (B2); Eleutherna, Crete (B3-B5, B7, B8, and El); Hipponion, Italy (B10); central Sicily (B11); and Pherai, Thessaly (Ph) share common formulas and also differ in their invocations to specific deities. Further methods in classifying the lamellae

---

[116] O. Kern, *Orphicorum Fragmenta* (Berolini: Apud Weidmannos, 1922). Also: G. Zuntz, *Persephone: Three Essays on Religion and Thought in Magna Graecia* (Oxford: Clarendon Press, 1971).

[117] R. Edmonds, *Roads Not Taken: Explorations of the 'Orphic' Gold Tablets* (Unpublished transcript from the Chicago Humanities Institute, University of Chicago, 1997). p. 19. Received by Prof. Albert Henrichs, spring 2003.

[118] Tzifopoulos, Yannis Z. *The Dionysiac(-Orphic) Lamellae of Crete*: With Contributions on the Archaeological Context by Irene Gavrilaki, Stella Kalogeraki, Eyrydiki Kefalidou, Popi Galanaki and Giorgos Rethemiotakis. (Unpublished manuscript given to me by Professor Yannis Z. Tzifopoulos, University of Crete, 2003) 21-22.

center on their treatment of eschatological beliefs and instructions to the soul within the texts. Some of the B group lamellae instruct the soul to write a prescribed formulary often ending with the inclusion of "passwords" and secret codes whose use supports the existence of an Orphic doctrine of recollection. The Timpone tablets (A1, A2, A3) from Thurii are so similar that their style could have originated from a single author. These three examples bring the initiate (or the deceased) to the forefront of this ritual context, speaking in the first person: "Pure I come from the pure, Queen of those below the earth."[119] If, on the other hand, these 'leaves' had multiple authors, then their transcription may have originated from a number of manuscripts. The same argument can be made from two tablets from different regions, namely the B1 (Petelia, Italy) and B2 (Pharsalos, Thessaly) examples that bear striking similarity in content and style. Examples such as the A and B tablets have been the source of debate for the following reasons.[120] First, their variety has served to perpetuate the argument that 'Orphics' have no organized social structure or unified beliefs that can be called 'Orphic'. In this ongoing discussion of an 'Orphic religion', Walter Burkert agrees with this belief by

---

[119] Edmonds, 13.

[120] Riedweg is skeptical that all of the lamellae can be classified within an "A" group. In this, Riedweg finds that A3's fragmentary nature (filled with erroneous phrases) lends itself to poor interpretation, for "Plotins gehört zu haben, wimmelt es doch teilweise von Schreibfehlern und Verstößen gegen die Metrik." (p. 363). Riedweg seems to argue that A3's translation / interpretation depends too much on A1 and A2 whose phrases were carelessly constructed. For an updated discussion on the accuracy of these translations, including a discussion on the author of these tablets, see C. Riedweg, "Initiation Tod Unterwelt: Beobachtungen zur Kommunikationssituation und narrativen Technik der Orphisch-Bakschischen Goldblattchen" in *Ansichten Griechischer Rituale: Geburtstags-Symposium fur Walter Burkert* (Stuttgart: B.G. Teubner, 1998): 362-364. While the philologists continue to debate these issues, it is my contention that such translations, while problematic in some areas, have provided us with insight into the Orphic ideas of the afterlife, specifically regarding the chthonic Olympian dichotomy which seems to pervade the texts on these tablets.

stating that "La critica ha giustamente sostenuto che non esisteva un « orfismo » come religione vera e propria, con determinati dogmi ed una organizzazione sopraregionale."[121] Secondly, the invocation, or more specifically the Persephone formula, becomes interchangeable among the tablets. Reference to her is prolific among the A tablets, while the B lamellae make no specific reference to this deity. In attempting an interpretation of the A tablets, we may come to equate the "Queen" of the Underworld with Persephone, and rightfully so. Only in A1 do we see the absence of an explicit Persephone formula: the goddess is otherwise invoked as the "Mistress" or "Queen." The A groupings stress an identification with the Goddess from below, the Queen, or Persephone. Thirdly, the multiple references to chthonic deities have proved it difficult to determine what was the pantheon of core deities. References to the Earth, the Heavens, and the Sun often suggests that the Orphics were divided in their religious affiliations. The issue here is not to distinguish polytheism from monotheism but to frame these issues in a broader context of theological syncretism.[122] Putting aside these textual differences, the thematic similarities among the tablets tend to support the thesis that Orphics were more organized than previously thought. Should these gold lamellae have been patterned from a 'corpus' of manuscripts, then the lines of transmission from region

---

[121] W. Burkert, "Le Laminette auree: da Orfeo a Lampone" in *Orfismo in Magna Grecia: Atti del quattordicesimo Convegno di Studi sulla Magna Grecia,* (Arte Tipografica: Napoli, 1975): 83.

[122] In Col. XXII of the Derveni Papyrus, the commentator addresses the multiplicity of deities and their relevance to the nature of men so that "Earth (Gŵ), Mother (Mŵtŵr), Rhea, and Hera are one and the same. She was called Earth (Gŵ) by convention; Mother, because all things are born from her; Gŵ and Gaia, according to each one's dialect. She was named Demeter, just like Gŵ- mŵtŵr: one name from both, for it was the same. And it is said in the Hymns too: Demeter Rhea Gŵ Mŵtŵr Hestia Dio." See: Andre Laks & Glenn W. Most "A Provisional Translation of the Derveni Papyrus". In: *Studies on the Derveni Papyrus.* (Oxford: Clarendon Press, 1997) p. 20.

to region could point to a more interconnected network of groups within the Orphic-Dionysian tradition.

What then, distinguishes the A tablets from their B counterparts? How is it that they have become classified into their separate groups, aside from the fact that Group B were found in Thessaly, Petelia, Crete, and Sicily? First, the soul is transported into the halls of Hades, the netherworld/underworld that symbolically represents the beginning of this afterlife journey. In this respect, some differences do exist. For example, B1[123] comes from Petelia, now modern Strongoli, 70 km south east of Thurii and 22 km north of Crotone. Plaque No. 3155 (B1) now in the British Museum, lies under the heading "Gold chain with amulet case." The gold plaque or lamella was folded up four times and placed within the pentagonal cylinder. It appears that since the gold plate would not fit after it was folded, one of the corners was cut off before placing it within the cylinder. This careless action resulted in the loss of four lines within the inscription. Interest in B1 often defers to the plaque itself, with no mention of it functioning as a necklace or amulet. Hanging from the cylinder is a chain with:

> 8-shaped links of double wire with hook and eye at either end respectively. On the chain is suspended a long pentagonal cylinder closed at one end, to the top of which two grooved rings are soldered. The chain passes through these rings. With

---

[123] Rendering a complete interpretation of B1 remains difficult and problematic. Lines 13: "?write this?" and 14: "?? Shadow covering around" are fragmentary and if preserved would have given us a better idea of the overall text. If, the sentence "write this" were an instruction for the soul or initiate then it would be consistent with the the Ph Group (Pherai, Thessaly) of unknown date; in this instance the text translates "Passwords: Male child of the thyrso, Male child of the thyrsos; Brimo, Brimo; Enter the sacred meadow. For the Initiate is without penalty." Line 19 of B11 also states "Passwords: Ph" which is then broken off. Could line 13 of B1 included a similar password as in the Ph example? Translation from Edmonds, 18.

the cylinder was found a tablet of very thin gold of oblong shape, cut away in two places below.[124]

In 1882 Smith and Comparetti published a new translation that expands on the initial publication of the tablet by Franz in 1836.[125] Line 13 of the Petelia tablet has been scrutinized for a number of reasons. First, since these gold tablets were either folded, rolled up or suffered damage by other agencies, inscriptions become difficult to translate.[126] Pointing to an earlier omission from Line 13, Smith states that:

> No one seems to hitherto have noticed that there has been a thirteenth line, written
> from bottom to top of the right edge of the plate; the fact that this line frequently
> encroaches more or less on the space allotted to the main inscription, has been one
> cause of uncertain readings with Kaibel and others: e.g. line 6, α‟τῷρ ἡμloὴ; line 7,
> є‑μ‑ αặlη; line 10, Ερόlєσσιν. I have been unable to reconstruct this line, owing to
> the crowded arrangement of some letters and the loss of others where the gold has
> been worn flat; but the final word seems tolerably certain.[127]

The inscription, now in the British Museum's Greek and Roman jewellery collection, begins by directing the soul in Hades to a spring on the left. This is contrasted with texts

---

[124] F.H. Marshall, M.A., *Catalogue of the Jewellery, Greek, Etruscan, and Roman, In the Departments of Antiquities, British Museum.* (London : Printed by order of the Trustees, 1911) 380.

[125] G. Franz. *Bulletino dell' Instituto di Corr. Arch, 1836,* p. 149.

[126] Further difficulties reside in the facsimiles of the B1 given to Franz and Smith upon which these translations have been based. In the 1836 and 1882 publications, any conclusions of the text and its relation to Orphic beliefs were viewed as preliminary and subject to human error. Recent translations like that of Edmonds (quoted earlier) have confirmed the authenticity of line 13.

[127] Cecil Smith and D. Comparetti, "The Petelia Gold Tablet," *The Journal of Hellenic Studies* 3 (1882): 113. A continuation of line 13 from the bottom to the top right edge of the plate is unique among the texts on gold lamellae and raises interesting questions. Either the inscriber ran out of space or line 13 was intentionally executed to set the password apart from the rest of the text. Lines 1-11 may represent part I of the formula whereby the soul becomes immortal by the permission of the chthonic deities and guardians of Mnemosyne. Lines 12-14 or Part II of the text exhibits a shift in emphasis so that the initiate must speak passwords (symbola) in order to complete the final phase of immortality.

like B2 (Pharsalos, Thessaly; now in the Museum of Volos, Inv. # M 65) circa 350-320

B.C. through B11, that locate the spring on the right side. If directing the soul in this

afterlife ritual was so important, one wonders why some of the tablets differ from one

another. Because of the similarities, it is probable that an oral tradition existed between

regional cults, so that knowledge would be kept among the priesthood. If this difference

cannot be attributed to such a mistake, then the possibility of multiple 'manuscripts'

remains open.

The Earth and Starry Heaven Formula

In all of the B tablets, there is the defining presence of a 'glowing cypress tree'

which sits beside the spring of Lethe (forgetfulness). A sacred cypress[128] tree, is

recognized and given importance as a marker in this transitory period for the soul. The

spring near this cypress is not to be touched or approached; its water is to be avoided at

all costs. Instead, the soul is advised to approach the lake of Memory, guarded by

daemons. As previously stated, the B tablets contain no specific references to

Persephone. In this case, the Persephone Formula is replaced by the proclamation "I am

the child of Earth and starry Heaven."[129] The scribe or priest finds it necessary to

enumerate the chthonic deities who are to be addressed by the initiate in a formal

manner. In some of the other B examples, "child" is interchangeable with "son" and

"daughter", but the main concept remains consistent throughout this classification.

---

[128] Pythagoras is said to have forbade that a coffin "be made of cypress-wood, either because the sceptre of Zeus is made of cypress, or for some other secret reason." Iamblichus, 69.
[129] Edmonds, 15-17.

The longest and oldest gold leaf (B10, Now in the State Archaeological Museum in Vibo, Inventory # not documented) was first discovered in a woman's grave, in the Locrian colony of Hipponium, which was founded around 600 B.C. A derivation of the Earth and starry Heaven formula can be found in line 10 of the Hipponion tablet (late fifth century B.C., Italy):

εἶπον· ''ἇς Γας ε–μι καὶ Οὐρανοῦ ἀστερόεντος·[130]

Say: "I am the child of Barea and starry Heaven[131]

Compare the Hipponion lamella with a third century B.C. hymn to Demeter, and we find that:

Ζε˜ς δ' ὑλαχεν Κρον–δης μῆγαν Οὐρανον ἀστερᾷεντα
ᾦεν–αν ἐν' ὑχηι βασιλε–αν·

Zeus, the son of Cronus, won the wide starry heaven to hold forever
as his kingdom.[132]

Here the initiate is tracing his/her lineage to the favorable chthonic deities of Earth and Heaven. Most likely Barea, a name exclusively used in this context, represents the personification of Earth and not the subterranean deity Persephone. Also worth noting is the absence of other chthonic deities such as Night, Uranos, or Oceanus. Nor is there any mention of the beginning of creation brought on by Chaos. Since the initiate is paying homage to the ancestors of Zeus, than would starry heaven be a metaphor for the universal order imposed by night? Is starry heaven the father of Uranos and Cronos/Kronos? Because of the spatial limitations afforded by the lamellae, their

---

[130] G. Pugliese Carratelli, "Un Sepolcro di Hipponion e un Nuovo Testo Orfico", Parola del Passato 29, 1974; 108.
[131] Edmonds, 10 & 17, respectively.
[132] Anonymous, "Select Papyri: Vol. III," Trans. D. L. Page (Cambridge, Massachusetts: Harvard University Press, 1970) 408-409.

respective authors had to be selective in their use of hexameter verse. Also, the use of "Barea" over other analogous symbols such as Demeter, Rhea, Mother Earth, Ge, Hestia or Deo may be attributed to preferences of anonymity in which initiates were required to have special knowledge of regional deities. A direct connection with Hesiod may prove useful, especially with respect to this idea of Earth as a primary force in the cycle of life: "Earth bore first of all one equal to herself, starry Heaven, so that he should cover her all about, to be a secure seat for ever for the blessed gods."[133] It is also likely that "Barea," in all of its obscurity, represents a regional deity comparable to the ones just mentioned.[134] Could this name simply represent a mystic symbol identifiable only by initiates inducted into this tradition at Hipponium?

The Concept of Memory

To drink from the lake of Memory ensures that the initiate will not only walk among the bacchics "βάχχοι" and initiates "στ εί χουσι" (B10, 16) but enter their prestigious ranks. As already shown, the lake or spring to be avoided can be found near the cypress tree. This, presumably, is Lethe, or the lake of Forgetfulness. To ignore the instructions inscribed onto this golden foil would end in the demise of the *Teletai* and

---

[133] Hesiod, *Theogony and Works and Days* Trans. M.L. West. (Oxford: Oxford University Press, 1988) 6.

[134] Giangrande's comprehensive philological study of the Hipponion lamellae points out some of the issues in translating this text. G. cannot be certain that the text is derived from a regional Doric dialect. G. also raises the possibility that the Hipponion text may represent a unique mixture of Doric and foreign elements. If Giangrande's proposition is correct, than it may explain, in part, the use of "Barea" as an artificial word specific to this region. See: Giuseppe Giangrande, "La lamina orfica di Hipponion" in Agostino Masaracchia., ed., *Orfeo e l'orfismo: Atti del Seminario Nazionale* (Roma: Gruppo Editoriale Internazionale, 1993) 235-236.

presumably result in rebirth of the soul into another living being. In the Hipponion tablet,
Lethe is not mentioned, so its name is only speculative at the moment. The lake of
Memory, on the other hand, is mentioned four times in the text and is thus translated:

Μνημοσῃ νας ῷπ͵ λίμνας (B10, 12 & 14)[135]

The lake of Memory, literally translated as Mnemosyne, represents the
cornerstone of this tablet. In order for the neophyte to enter the ranks of *mystai*, he/she
must correctly identify its location and drink from it. The leaf inscription begins on the
first line with an emphasis on memory:

1 Μναμοσύνας τᾷδε ὑργον.ἤπεὴ ὼν μήλληισι θανε͏σθαι[136]

1 Μναμοσύνας τᾷδε <h>.ιερᾷν· ἤπεὴ ὠμ μήλληισι θανε͏σθαι
This is the <sacred> of memory. When you are about to die...[137]

As we can see from line 1 from Hipponion, the Orphic conception of memory can be
translated in different ways. Either "Μναμοσύνας" refers to the lake (Mnemosyne), an
armor to be worn by the soul, or the tablet itself. Edmonds translates <h>ιερᾷν· in B10,
1 as "the <sacred?> of Memory"[138] while Giangrande translates ϋϱ-ον in B10, 1 as
"sepolcro" or "tomba."[139] Giangrande essentially compares this first line from Hipponion
to fragments 32 g3 in Kern to show that line 1 is referencing the gold tablet as a tomb in

---

[135] Edmonds, 11.

[136] C. G., Pugliese "Un Sepolcro di Hipponion e un Nuovo Testo Orfico", Parola del
Passato 29, 1974. 108.

[137] Edmonds, 11 and 17, respectively.

[138] Edmonds, 11.

[139] Giangrande, 242-244.

itself, the holder of memory. The gold tablet, therefore, documents itself as the initiatory tomb of the individual passing onto the netherworld; its self-referentiality[140] is not so much a testament to outside individuals as it is an instructional note to the neophyte who must preserve previous memories in order to walk among the pure. The text has been written on the gold foil so that it may be read again in the afterlife by the soul who has (we assume) already prepared for this journey. Whether or not we can accept Edmonds and Giangrande's translations may be left for future research. It is clear that the Hipponion gold leaf functioned as a ritual instrument to be read upon the journey of the soul to the netherworld. Further support for a doctrine of metempsychosis can be shown, for it is the prohibition against forgetfulness that lends credence to this lamellae; the Hipponion tablet is attempting to prevent the return of the soul to a lower plane of existence. Tablet B11 from central Sicily of the third century B.C. is strikingly similar to B10, maintaining the first line as a reference to itself as a testament to memory while making some additions to the form as outlined in the Hipponion formulas. B1 from Petelia preserves a similar proclamation as a testament or signifier to memory, but in the 12th line, while B10 and B11 use it in line 1. Instructions to write a formulary are given in (B1, 13) and in line 2 of B11.

The oblong lamellae of thin gold (A5), acquisition No. 3154 in the British Museum, was inscribed with Greek cursive letters and dates from the second through third centuries A.D. It was found near San Paolo Fuori le Mura near Rome and was acquired by the British Museum in 1899. F. H. Marshall's analysis of A5 in the Catalogue of Greek, Etruscan, and Roman Jewellery in the British Museum relies heavily

---

[140] Perhaps the first line referencing itself may have read "This is the <sacred path> of memory" or "This is the <sacred amulet> required of memory."

on a symbolic interpretation of the Petelia tablet's (B1) references to memory. Although A5 dates from the later period of the Roman empire in which Gnostic inscriptions are more prevalent, it retains much of the language that connects Bacchica and Orphica allegiances to Persephone, Zeus, and presumably the child-king "Ε̤κεεϲ Ε̂βουλλ̇ε τε (A5,1)."[141] Contention regarding A5,3 as a gift of memory is compared against the allusion in B1,12 to Μνημοσ̄νας. Is the inscription of Μνημοσ̄νας in both A5 and B1 referring to 1) the amulet as a token of memory, or 2) the waters of lake Mnemosyne?

Entrance To Immortality

Previously we had discussed the possibility that A5's "gift" was in fact a *Memoriae arma* to protect the patron Caecilia Secundina. The value of the Petelia tablet must not be understated. Marshall's publication of A5 depends extensively on the interpretations of B1. The British Museum study's comparison with B1 shows that A5 is citing Caecilia Secundina as the patron, and Memory (Μνημοσ̂νης) as signifying the water in the underworld instead of the amulet itself (see Giangrande's argument on the lamellae as a metaphor for "tomba.") Since A5 dates from the later period, it represents an abbreviated formula from its predecessors. Also, this plate from Rome diverges from custom since Caecilia Secundina enters the ranks of godhead and not the traditional entrance to *mystai* or *bacchoi* as found in the other tablets herein discussed. It is here that ancient beliefs in metempsychosis and immortality not only converge but become difficult to disentangle. Whether memory is embodied in the water of afterlife or was believed to embody the

---

[141] Edmonds, 4.

amulet remains an open discussion. The initiate is protecting himself/herself against something, by being buried with an amulet made of an enduring material that will transmit the necessary formulas to avoid Lethe or forgetfulness. A5 certainly attests to the human belief in divine ascension, a trait not necessarily characteristic of Orphic practices from the classical period throughout Thessaly and Magna Graecia.

Can these differences in arrangement be chance occurrences related to an oral tradition or intentional transcriptions by the respective communities of Hipponion, Petelia and the provinces of Rome? The transmission of a supposed instructional manuscript, if it originated in fifth century B.C. Hipponion, may have eventually made its way down to Petelia[142] where its form became altered. The second line in B11 appears to be an instruction for the soul to write a formula upon death, expanding upon the idea that such lamellae were to be used in further ritual contexts beyond the material realm. Whereas in the Hipponion formula, Barea is used as the divinized parent, B11 reverts to the Earth and starry Heaven formula, declaring lineage as a qualification for the soul to enter beyond this material realm and into timelessness. B11, in all of its grandeur and proclamations of purity, presents us with some interesting questions that need to be addressed. First, is the gold leaf commentator instructing the departed soul to write down instructions during this initial part of the journey or is it more of an exercise in memory? If the former is the case, then the gold lamellae can be seen in the context of instructional

---

[142] The social, religious and economic ties to mystery cults of this southern colony are strengthened by Petelia's distance of 30 kilometers from Croton. The Pythagoreans were very active in the politics of Croton, and held strong onto their position until their banishment from the city in the late sixth century B.C. Influence of this sort may have broader implications in and around Petelia, and may suggest a stronger influence between the Pythagoreans and Orphics than previously thought. This northern town would have been the perfect resettlement for exiled Pythagorean loyalists who would have been qualified scribes of the golden lamellae.

notes toward creating an amulet for the soul. It also subsumes a hierarchical system of authority by which the *magoi* or scribe of the lamellae speaks beyond this world and assumes direction over the pupil who is deceased. Second, how can this issue of written versus mental ritual instructions reflect on Orphic conceptions of post-mortem ritual? If such knowledge as preserved in the golden lamellae were first learned by the *teletai* in preparation for their own death, then the possibility of a mimetic enactment (the death of Dionysus or the abduction of Persephone) in Orphic ritual practices remains a strong possibility. At first glance, one may be tempted to further divide B10 and B11 in alternate groupings, solely based on their thematic and textual divergences. B11 exhibits further complications owing to the incompleteness of the text in lines 19-21. What we are left with most likely represents further instructions and the use of "Passwords" of "Ph" and "Phe" with the remainder of the formula cut off. It is quite possible that the password spelled out Persephone, the queen of the underworld who was coupled with her underworld consort. Persephone appears in the second century B.C. tablet from Eleutherna (El) and remains a constant theme in Orphic theology.

Burial Finds

Perhaps the most difficult part in piecing together data from these gold foils is their lack of context. The destruction and looting of grave-goods, well documented throughout the centuries, has been a primary concern among all archaeologists. In most instances, the lack of archaeological data and the migration of objects from their original place of burial, has limited our understanding of what their function was, who it was intended for, and its overall historical, social and material context. Notwithstanding, the most detailed archaeological site report among the A and B groupings can be found in the 1879 excavations of the Timpone Tumuli which uncovered five well-preserved lamellae. Francesco Saverio Cavallari (1809-1896) began his search among four round elevations thought to be the necropolis of Thurii. Located in the present day Calabrian city of Sibari, the Timpone site lies just south of the river Crati (the ancient Krathis) and 4 km north of the tributary Coscile. Thurii had been founded by Athenians and exiled Sybarites in 444 B.C. on the site of Sybaris, which in turn was founded by the Achaeans in 720 B.C. Sybaris may have had close ties with its surrounding neighbors, particularly Croton, since the latter was founded by the Achaeans in 708 B.C. The landscape had been transformed over the years, with power changing hands in a six hundred-year period. Thurii was defeated by the Lucanians in 390 B.C. and saw its eventual defeat in 212 B.C. in its revolt against the Romans. The final ancient settlement to have been founded was the Latin colony Copia in 193 B.C.

Cavallari first encountered the Timpone Paladino, located north of the other three tumuli. After finding shards of "vasi finissimi con pitture del V secolo,"[143] there, he decided to begin excavating the Timpone Grande. Cavallari's drawings (Fig. 4.) of the Timpone Grande at Thurii, reflect his dedication to measuring topographical elements and documenting the stratigraphy of the necropolis. Measuring 28 meters in diameter and 9 1/2 meters in height, the Timpone Grande contained eight main strata, with layers of earth, ash, carbon and pebbles each a half meter thick. The repeated layering, according to Cavallari, attests to the sacrifices and libations purportedly carried out over the

---

[143] Cavallari, *Notizie degli Scavi di Antichita*. (Rome: Accademia Nazionale dei Lincei, 1879) 217.

deceased's grave. Plant roots, flowers, and shards of burnt vases were among the layered

finds. The oblong tomb, built from large tufa blocks, measured 30 cm high, 1/2 meter

thick, and was oriented towards the bottom center proper of the Timpone tumulus. Three

slabs (26.5 cm) covered the tomb, with detailing of a possible temple on the edges

visible. Having found the skeleton (gender not documented) in the coffin facing east,

Cavallari turned his attention to two silver medallions decorated with female heads near

the chest proper. The grave also contained two small wooden boxes stylized with inlaid

palmettes and some tiny pieces of gold.[144]

Examination of the head revealed two inscribed gold lamellae which lay close to

it, each folded nine times over. When it was unwrapped, much to Cavallari's

astonishment, he found two lamellae, with A4 (measuring 54 X 29 mm) inside lamellae

C (81 X 23 mm). Folded in somewhat envelope-fashion, A4 (National Museum of

Naples, Inventory # 111463) reads:

'Αλλ' ἀπᾷταν ψυχῈ προλ‒πηι φῶος ᾠελ‒οιο,
δεξι͙ν Ε.ΘΙΑΣ δ' ᾐξι. <έ>ναι πεφυλαγμῆνον ε μϚλα πϚντα·
χα‒ρε παθ͙ν τ͙ πϚθημα τ͙ δ' ο͙πω πρᾳσθ'{ε} ἠπεπᾴνθεις·

---

[144] Unfortunately, no drawings or other reproductions of the coins and small wooden boxes have been found. Zuntz, 1971 states that the coins may have depicted Aphrodite, Persephone or the "city goddess of Thurii (in a similar style to the 'Arethusa' on Syracusan coins)," P. 290. One of the tombs also contained a fourth century B.C. Apulian vase painting depicts Hekate who sits in judgement along with her consort Pluto/Hades. Eurydice, although depicted in this scene, is unlikely to be depicted on these burial coins. Not all females portrayed would have deity status. In the red-figure vase dating from 440-430 B.C., we see a muse carrying a lyre (Lexicon Iconographicum Mythologiae Classicae, No. 68). In an Apulian volute crater from 330 B.C., Orpheus and Eurydice stand before Hekate, Persephone, Hades, while Eros is represented standing next to an unidentified female figure (L.I.M.C., No. 80). Again caution must be exercised, for such identification presupposes a link between the coins and the gold leaves found with the skeleton.

θε˙ͅς ἠγένου ἠξ ὦνθρῖπου· ὑριφος ἠς γῶλα ὑπετες.
χα→ρ<ε> χα→ρε· δεξιῶν ᾀδοιπᾀρ<εἠ̃>
λειμ˙νζς θ᾿{ε} ἀεροις καὴ ὠλσεα Φερσεφονε‒ας.[145]

1   But when the soul leaves the light of the sun,
2   Go straight to the right, having kept watch on all things very well.
3   Hail, you having experienced the experience. This you had not experienced before.
4   A god you have become from a man. A kid you fell into milk.
5   Hail, hail; making your way to the right,
6   The sacred meadows and groves of Phersephoneia.[146]

Before we address the significance of Tablet A4, some comments on C are in order. As far as accurate and clear translations are concerned, no definitive reproduction of tablet C is available aside from the collection of words compiled by Jane Ellen Harrison. Measuring 2 cm in height, and comprised of ten lines of writing, much of the text is unrecognizable. Folding of the gold tablet, as we have shown, resulted in a number of creases, cracks, and scratches to the surface- all of which compromised the translation and reproduction of the inscription. In an ambitious effort to expound upon the translations of Kern (1922) publication of *Orphicorum Fragmenta*, and Barnabei's *Lamellae aureae Orphicae*, Zuntz (1971) argues that "The fact that no coherent reconstruction is possible on a basis as corrupt as this. The suggestions underneath my transcript do indeed show that more Greek words can be elicited from this jumble than might be expected from first sight."[147] Zuntz's argument is furthered by his suspicion that "the wording was intentionally made incomprehensible, in order to enhance its magic

---

[145] D. Comparetti, "Sibari," *Notizie degli Scavi* 3 (1879): 156

[146] Edmonds, 14.

[147] Zuntz, 350.

power; but the sequences of meaningless letters bear no similarity to the well-known methods of magical abracadabras, 'Ephesia Grammata', or secret codes."[148] Based on the writings of all these authors, two possibilities remain: either the author of C was intentionally misleading the reader (the initiate) as to keep the lamella secret among initiates of the order, or the scribe made numerous errors in transcribing the Greek, being more accustomed to his native Italic language; this may also support the existence of an original manuscript that the scribe had access to. The latter explanation is further supported by numerous instances in which the repetition of sequences are shown to repeat the same kind of grammatical and spelling mistakes. The author intentionally intersperses Doric, Hexameter, and traditional epic forms throughout C. We must not forget the damage incurred by multiple creases, folding of the gold material, scratches and wear that compromised the integrity of the text. Notwithstanding the conclusions that tablet C is "incomprehensible," an attempt to extrapolate the text and forward some comparisons with regards to A4 seems appropriate since both were folded into one another. Harrison (1922) compiled an impressive collection of Orphic divinities from tablet C (National Museum of Naples, Inventory # 111464):

Πρωτογᾶνω<ι> ΤΗΜΑΙΤΙΕΤΗ Γα, ι ματρ– ΕΠΑ Κυβελε–α <ι> Κᾶ-
ρρα <ι> ΟΣΕΝΤΑΙΗ Δϋμητρος ΗΤ
ΤΑΤΑΙΤΤΑΤΑΠΤΑ Ζε☐ ΙΑΤΗΤΥ ᾤ̀ηρ ΣΑΠΤΑ Ἥλιε, πυρ δϋ
πῷντα ΣΤΗΙΝΤΑΣΤΗΝΙΣΑΤΟΠΕ νικαι Μ
ΣΗΔΕ Τ῀χα ΙΤΕ φῷνης, πῷμνηστοι Μοῆρα ι ΣΣΤΗΤΟΙΓΑΝΝΥΑ-
ΠΙΑΒΤΗ σ῀ κλυτὴ δαιμον ΔΕΥΧΙ
Σ πῷτερ ΑΤΙΚ παντοδαμῷστα ΠΑΝΤΗΡΝΥΝΤΑΙΣΕΛΑΒΔΟΝΤΑ-
ΔΕΠ ᾤνταμοιβϋ ΣΤΛΗΤΕΑΣΤΑ
ΤΗΜΗ ᾤ̀ηρ Ι πυρ ΜΕΜ Μῷτερ ΛΥΕΣΤΙΣΟΙΛ-ΕΝΤΑΤΟ Νόστι Ν
ν῀ξ ΙΝΗΜΕΦ ϋμῆρα ΜΕΡΑΝΕΓΛΧΥΕΣ
ᾖπτημαρ ΤΙ νϋστιας ΤΑΝ Ζε☐ ἠνορ῀ττιε(?) καὴ πανᾶπτα. α–ῆν

---

[148] Zuntz, 345.

```
ΑΙΜΙΥ* ματερ, ἡμας ἠπ-
ῴκουσον ΕΟ ευχας ΤΑΚΤΑΠΥΑΡΣΥΟΛΚΑΠΕΔΙΩΧΑΜΑΤΕΜΑΝ
    καλ{η}ῷ Δ ερῷ ΔΑΜΝΕΥΔΑΜΝΟΙ
ΩΤΑΚΤΗΡ ερῷ ΜΑΡ Δημότερ, πρ, Ζε, Κᾷρη Χθονα
    ΤΡΑΒΔΑΗΤΡΟΣΗΝΙΣΤΗΟΙΣΤΝ
ἔρως ΝΗΓΑΥΝΗ φῶς ἧς φρενα ΜΑΤΑΙΜΗΤΝΝΤΗΣΝΥΣΧΑ
    μῦστωρ ἐ᾿λε Κο῾ρην
α᾿α φΗΡΤΟΝΟΣΣΜΝΟ-ΕΣΤΟΝ ῷῆρ ΤΑΙΠΛΝΙΛΛΥ ἧς φρενα
ΜΑΡ*ΤΩΣ[149]
```

"O first-born, Earth, Counsellor, All-Motherly, Cybelean, Kora, Holy Child of Demeter(?)......, All-Seeing Zeus, Healer, and thou Sarapis, Sun, Fire-Kindler, Maker-of-Appearances, Far-Seeing(??)

Victory and equal Fortune; come ye, Phanes, All-Counselling Fates (or With victories and Fortunes thou didst appear, with the All-Devising Fates)

Stayers(?), All-Accomplishers(?), Well-named Daemon, Master, Healer(?), All-Subduer, All-Controller, Driver of Thunder, Sickle-Bearer(?)......to be endured in all wise. That thou mayest not with vapour make to burn a tumour in me (??)... I will pay ... sevenfold fasting. In the nights or after daybreak I ... for seven days the fasting.

Zeus Penetrator (?) and All-seeing, Divine, Ruler of Streams, ... ye will make to spring a stream not in drops of fire ......

Plain ... guide ... Divine Rhadamanthys[150] ... for six days ... Zeus ... Demeter ... Healer, Sun ...   that she share the Shrine for five days may not ...."[151]

To dismiss C altogether would be an injustice to the findings; tablet C was not classified with the A grouping precisely because it lacks the directional instructions (and formulas) frequently found in Thessaly, Crete, or Italy. In concurrence with G. Zunt's statement that the text hints of "philosophical allegorism,"[152] tablet C can be shown to

[149] D. Comparetti, "Sibari," *Notizie degli Scavi* 3 (1879): 329.

[150] For commentary on Rhadamanthus as one of the judges in the afterlife see Plato, "Euthyphro, Apology, Crito, Phaedo, Phaedrus," Trans. Harold North Fowler (Cambridge, Massachusetts: Harvard University Press, 2001) 143.

[151] Harrison, 666. Harrison was the only scholar who attempted an English translation of an otherwise difficult text.

[152] Zuntz, 351. Allegory can express a narrative, painting or story by using symbolic figures or in the case of this lamella, mythological characters. Reincarnation, therefore, can be expressed by depicting a complex and intricate narrative of Greek divinities who

reflect beliefs in metempsychosis just as its A4 counterpart will illustrate. Two of the references to deities, "All-Motherly" and "Kora" (C, 1) that have been reconstructed in C, reflect the importance of the mother so that "everything is inferior to Demeter."[153] In this first reconstructed phrase, the recurring deities in this afterlife drama, Demeter and Kore, are mentioned together. Regarding the second phrase, a thrice pronounced invocation[154] is dedicated to Zeus (C, 11), Demeter (C, 12), and Helios (C, 2 and 14)[155]. Hellenic mystery cults, it has been shown, held varying theological interpretations regarding their deity of choice.[156] If, as the text states, Demeter is superior to the other

---

are sometimes referred to by abstract concepts like the Maker-of-Appearances (C, 3) who is all-knowing Zeus.
[153] Zuntz, 350.

[154] In the first book of Plato's Republic and Timaeus, Proclus sites three different formula in three citations to address the doctrine κατατ αρτῷρῶσις, which concerns "the works of Orphics." In like fashion, tablets P1 and P2 from Pelinna, Thessaly announce the soul as having been died and born "thrice blessed one on this day." (Edmonds, 14).

[155] In a cautious attempt to relate these findings to specific acts of worship, the lamellae should not be viewed as evidence of sun worship, rather, they point to the intricate and complex association of the sun to cosmogonic theory. The Derveni Papyrus outlines six commentaries in which the sun is predominant, and is the cause of both Divine and Mortal creation. Columns IV, XIII, XIV, XV, XVI, and XXV, respectively, show that the sun has creative power as in the case of Kronos who was born to the Earth from the sun (Col. XIV) and to the creation of "things" by god (Col. XXV). (Laks and Most, 15 & 21). The sun, measuring in terms of a human foot in width, is given specific boundaries the likes of which are controlled by the Erinyes. Should the sun expand beyond its natural dimensions, this transgression of Justice is corrected by these primordial beings. This is substantiated by the words of the Pre-Socratic philosopher Heraclitus (Col. IV). The sun is described in terms of arch$\hat{\omega}$, or the beginning principle which created Kronos and Zeus. Once father and son had fought, the sun become divided and transformed the world into its present state of existence (Col. XV). We may view this transformation in terms of Dionysos' dismemberment, a horrific event that ultimately led to his ascension to immortality.

[156] Pythagoras taught that worshippers ought to perform three libations to the gods. Specific names are not given, nor are the ritual procedures outlined. In this same

deities, then why is the sun god mentioned before her? Part of this answer may lie in the multiplicity of devotional sects common among "Orphics."[157] Not all of the *magoi* associated with Orpheus would have prayed, worshipped or performed burial rites in the same way. Regional differences in burial rituals and beliefs in metempsychosis, particularly between tablets A4/C and B1, symbolizes their respective allegiances to deities. These differences may have stemmed from interpretations of cosmogonic events pertinent to the creation of man's soul. Also inscribed are the names for all-devising fate, the victories and fortunes, and allusions to fire and air. We are here reminded again by Col. XXII of the Derveni Papyrus in which the powers of Earth (Gŵ), Mother (Mŵtŵr), Rhea and Hera are equated with Demeter.[158] The Derveni text not only shows the importance of names, but their being created by the force that initiates all things into being, namely Zeus (otherwise known as Moira). Aside from representing mother Earth,

---

fragment, Apollo is said to give oracles from a tripod (three legs) because "number first came into being as a triad" (Cf. Iamblichus, 67).

[157] Not all ancient references refer to the worship of Dionysus as the primary concern among the Orphics. In a lost play by Aeschylus, Ps. Eratosthenes' work the *Catasterismi* states that Orpheus was purported to have ascended Mount Pangaeum to pay worship to the sun. Denying worship to Dionysos, Orpheus proclaimed the sun to be Apollo. In contrast, Macrobius' *Saturnalia* records Orpheus who proclaims Dionysos and Helios (sun) to be one and the same god and "described his vestements in the sacra Liberalia (item Orpheus Liberum atque Solem unum esse deum eundemque demonstrans de ornatu vestituque eius in sacris Liberalibus ita scribit" Eratosthenes. *Eratosthenis* "Catasterismorum Reliquiae : Accedunt Prologomena et Epimetra Tria" Trans. Carolus Robert (Berolini : Apud Weidmannos, 1963) 24. *Liberalibus* literally transcribed as "vestements used in the rites," may refer to the duality of Diononysos-Helios or the specific garments prescribed for burial (Woolen clothes were said to be forbidden material in the burials of Pythagoreans and Orphics alike. One is reminded of the pilgrimage whereby Orpheus travels to Mount Pangaion (the same as Mount Pangaeum cited by Ps. Eratosthenes?) where he learns the number theory theology taught by Pythagoras. Cf. Iamblichus, 65.

[158] Laks and Most, 20.

Demeter's association with the changing of the seasons represents a similar type of metempsychosis in which life changes from different forms.[159]

How, it may be asked, does tablet C from the Timpone Grande support the deceased's belief in metempsychosis? Tablet C, according to G. Zuntz, may consist of Kore's prayer to her mother Demeter.[160] Having been kidnapped by Hades, she seeks to live again. Living with her husband in the underworld is torture and represents a lower kind of existence. In the Rhapsodies, Zeus rapes both Rhea-Demeter and Kore, who are both in snake form. Since Tablet C, along with A4 was buried close to the head of this important individual, we can only speculate as to its function as a magical amulet to guide the soul in the afterlife. Having the Kore's prayer (C) would then enable the deceased to escape the wheel of life or reincarnation into human or other life body. The return to Earth, as in Kore's case, represents an interesting parallel to the soul of the deceased in the Timpone Grande who seeks renewed life among the gods. It is precisely this kind of association between religious symbolism and burial practice in the Timpone Grande that lends strength to ideas of metempsychosis in the gold leaves. The folding of the gold foils, nine times each in successive manner, coupled with joining of the texts, points to their being used as magical amulets for an afterlife journey. The invocation of

---

[159] In the last sentence of Col. XXII in the Derveni Papyrus, this idea of transformation and rebirth is shown by Rhea who is said give birth to animals and Demeter is transformed into Deio who "because she was cut (edŵiõthŵ) during sexual intercourse." (Laks and Most, 20).

[160] Rites, invocations and burial practices referring to Demeter Chthonia, Kore Soteira and Persephone would have relevance in this southern Italian province since Orpheus was said to found various Athenian and Spartan cults to these deities. Migration of these practices were common enough to find themselves in the form of Gold lamellae deposited in the Italic peninsula.

the names of divine beings, particularly in such a cryptic manner, lends further evidence

the possible existence of a sacred ritual meant to restore the soul to a higher realm of

being, a place that was meant to transcend the mortal realm of Earth. The invocation to

"sevenfold fasting" (C, 5 & 6), may not only refer to one's purity, but may document a

more general ritual that was enacted prior to the initiate's death.

Tablets A

With some of the problems and intricacies of tablet C having been discussed, A4

will be discussed both in its own context and in relation to its counterpart. Having sorted

both of the Timpone Grande tablets into different categories, one cannot forget that both

were used together as a single amulet. A4 was not only folded nine times but followed

the same folding that C had undergone: starting from the right side proper and ending in

shorter proportions to the left side proper.[161] The originality of A4 is quite astonishing.

Line 1 begins with:

Αλλ᾽ ἀπᾷ́ταν ψυχὲ προλπηι φῷος ῷελοιο,
But when the soul leaves the light of the sun,[162]

In all of the golden lamellae discussed thus far, none specifically reference the

sun in reference to the soul's journey. Instead of a solar reference, tablets A1-A3, A5 and

---

[161] There has been no discussion in any of the literature regarding the ritual decryption of C and A4 in their combined manner. Did the ritual of folding the lamellae into little "envelopes" involve a person beside the author? The deceased individual in the Timpone Grande would presumably have to 1) prepare the amulet for decryption, 2) carry the amulet into the afterlife, and 3) execute the formulary so as to achieve immortality. Perhaps tablet C was to be executed first, since it addresses cosmogonic events that have a direct bearing on mortality. A4 may have been the final step before achieving immortality.
[162] Edmonds, 14.

B1-B2 announce the soul's chthonic birth from the Queen below or her entrance into Hades. A4 is similar in respect to the other tablets (B2-B11), which direct the soul to the right path, shunning the left as a gateway back to mortality. The Derveni Papyrus has been extremely helpful in understanding ancient conceptions of cosmogony's relation to ritual practice and belief. Helios is at once the controlling factor and the beginning principle (archŵ) described in Col. XVI:

> Of the first-born king, the reverend one. And unto him all
> The immortals grew, blessed gods and goddesses
> And rivers and lovely springs and everything else
> That has been born then; and he himself was alone.[163]

The sun, being archŵ, is declared by Zeus as a genital organ or "*aidoion*" therefore, all things mortal and immortal usher forth from this *aidoion*. Further support for this belief can be found in Col. XIII, whereby Zeus likens the sun to *aidoion* because "men consider birth to be dependent upon the genitals."[164] Mortals, according to Zeus, are focused on the material realm and must be nurtured in this respect. When the soul departs from the sun in A4,1 there is a hint of commonality with the Derveni cosmogony. A4 illustrates the commonality of Mortals and Immortals since they both originate from the same source and may potentially end up together in the "end." A belief in metempsychosis is supported by A4 since the soul can either go to the right and achieve immortality or go to the left and return to its previous existence (or possibly into a lower form). The former scenario is contingent upon the soul having the memory to render the amulet useful towards this task. Memory and ritual preparation of the soul in his/her mortal existence is

---

[163] Laks & Most, 16.

[164] Laks & Most, 15. Interestingly, Zeus is said to have swallowed *aidoion* in Col. XIII. This may also reference Zeus' castration of Kronos and his subsequent rule of the universe. Refer back to tablet C in which Zeus and Helios are conjointly invoked.

what separated them from those who had no training in these mystical arts. Once the

initiate has followed the right path, they have "experienced the experience" and become a

god.[165] Still further, the soul becoming a god symbolizes a return to archŵ, a time when

both mortals and immortals were one with the sun. In another reference attributed to

Orpheus, it is not Persephone who intercedes but Justice who sits beside the throne of

Zeus and decides the fate of men.[166]

Now that the soul has become a god, line 4 pronounces "A kid you fell into

milk."[167] The mysterious nature of this phrase has caused much discussion, with little

conclusion as to its true meaning. First, there is no firm evidence that it references the

child Dionysos who is torn from the titans and is reborn into a god. Born from Semele or

by Persephone as a result of being raped by Zeus, the child must undergo death to

achieve kingship. Having been guarded by the dancing Korybantes, he is thus distracted

by the Titans and is torn to pieces. Falling into milk as a child may represent the rebirth

of the individual as Dionysos was born again and nursed by the nursing milk of

Persephone. Kore herself undergoes a similar type of metamorphosis by returning to

mother Demeter where corn is the fertile element.[168] We know from the Eleusinian

mysteries, that ritual death gives way to a divine birth. Here Demeter or Persephone,

---

[165] Executing both lamellae in a ritual sequence may have been necessary in order for the soul to achieve godhead. A4 and C appear as one and yet separate so that their decryption initiates the soul's ascension. The "experience" may refer to soul's mortal instruction as well as the post-mortem act of following the instruction.

[166] Demosthenes, "Orations XXI-XXVI," Trans. J. H. Vince (Cambridge, Massachusetts: Harvard University Press, 1998) 521.

[167] Edmonds, 14.

[168] Aelian, "Historical Miscellany (Varia Histirica)," Trans. N. G. Wilson (Cambridge, Massachusetts: Harvard University Press, 1997) 51. Julian, "The Works of the Emperor Julian: Vol. I," Trans. Wilmer Cave Wright (Cambridge, Massachusetts: Harvard University Press, 1962) 483.

most commonly known as the "Mistress," gives "birth to a sacred boy, Brimo the Brimos."[169] Looking back at the tablet from Pherai, Thessaly (unknown date), the passwords of Male child of the thyrsos and Brimo are instructed to enter the sacred meadow. Brimo is also another name for Hecate, queen of the dead who utilizes charms and drugs to perform spells over the troubled souls who pass through Hades.[170]

On April 9, 1879, Cavallari ended the excavation of the Timpone Piccolo owing to the impending malaria season. Had he continued his efforts, he would have found three more lamellae interred within the tumulus. Located 265 meters west of the Timpone Grande, the Timpone Piccolo's circumference measured 52 meters with a height of 5 meters. In the two strata measuring 60 cm there contained layers of Earth where "more than 10 persons were carelessly interred."[171] All of the bodies found in the Timpone Piccolo were inhumed, whereas evidence of cremated remains were deposited above the tomb in the Timpone Grande. The former burial mound revealed three tombs made from Tufa slabs, the same kind of material used in the one discovered by Cavallari. What the purpose of these cremated and inhumed burials above the two main strata was remains a mystery. Perhaps they represented sacred burial rites among the people of Thurii or as Zuntz suggests were used in times of epidemics.[172] A purpose of the Timpone Grande may have been forgotten by the local denizens and ultimately it may have been converted to a larger all-purpose burial ground. The Timpone Grande skeleton

---

[169] Burkert (1998), p. 288.

[170] Apollonius Rhodius, "The Argonautica," Trans. R. C. Seaton (Cambridge, Massachusetts: Harvard University Press, 1967) 253. Hecate or Brimo, is also the queen of the underworld, and is considered to be the nurse of youth. Could the Orphic lamellae be addressing Hecate when invoking Brimo?

[171] Zuntz, 291.

[172] Zuntz, 287.

lay facing east with the lamellae near the head. In similar fashion, the Timpone Piccolo

skeletons all lay facing in the same manner, but with the gold lamellae near the right

hand in each case. These similarities suggest contrasting approaches to ritual burial and

remain ellusive to our contemporary minds. Another troubling aspect to this evidence is

the absence of any reproductions of the accompanying grave goods owing to looting and

loss of the archaeological material through poor management of artifacts. For instance,

the Timpone Piccolo grave reportedly contained two small terracotta heads interred with

the skeleton (it is not known if they were placed inside or outside the coffin). These have

been missing since their transfer to the local municipality of Corregliano Calabro in

1880.[173] In contrast are the missing silver medallions with female heads found in the

Timpone Grande. The depositing of such female figure medallions seems to have

significance with regard to the golden lamellae, perhaps representing an affiliation with a

local goddess like Demeter, Kore or even Hera, all of whom are shown on a number of

Apulian vase paintings. Unfortunately, none of these medallions were described in the

excavation reports.

 Fortunately, all three lamellae in the Timpone Piccolo (National Museum of

Naples, Inventory #'s 111625, 111623, 111624) were preserved. Of the three tombs, the

first one revealed tablet A1, which is the most carefully written of all the Timpone

lamellae. The second tomb revealed A3 and the third A2. Another distinction between

the tumuli is evident: Whereas A1 and A3 were not folded (compared to the complexity

---

[173] Zuntz, 297. Also missing is a Lucanian plate, red on black, with a winged, hermaphroditic genius holding a wreath. This was reportedly found outside the third tomb in the Timpone Piccolo. Similar pieces of red-figure and black-varnished vase ware were found in the Timpone Grande, leading Cavallari to estimate the tomb from the fifth-fourth centuries B.C.

of A4/C), A2 was folded once. Obviously, folding of lamellae was not a common practice among the *orphikoi/magoi*, who would have differing opinions as to the importance of this practice. Turning now to the textual evidence, A1, A2, and A3 return again to the primordial mother, the "pure Queen," who sits in judgement of the soul in the underworld. Line 2 in all three lamellae invokes the names of Eukles and Eubouleus, which have a connection with Hades/Pluto, Zeus, Zagreus, Phanes[174], and Hades-Plouton. Eukles/Eubouleus[175] also refers to an epithet of Dionysos or the divine child, as evident from A5,2 (Rome, 260 A.D., British Museum, Inventory # 3154) that invokes:

Ἐκλεες Ἐβουλε τε Δι̇ς τῆκος· ϛλλῷ δῆχεσθεε[176]

"Eukles and Eubouleus, child of Zeus, radiant one."[177]

Here the suppliant must announce the reincarnation of the soul through the body of Persephone as the divine child of Dionysos. Being of the blessed race is not a hollow invocation, it allows the initiate to link myth with reality, and realize that his/her true lineage actually stems from the gods. It has been established that the Timpone Grande lamella closely affiliated itself with an Orphic theogony reminiscent of the Derveni Papyrus. This lies in stark contrast to those lamellae from the Timpone Piccolo. In the

---

[174] Phanes is referred to in the *Argonautica* and Orphic Hymns as the first king to usher from Aither and Chaos, the forces associated with the beginning of Greek primordial cosmogony. The many names of Phanes include Zeus, Bromios, Metis (tranformation of Zeus in Col. XV of the Derveni Papyrus), Protogonos, and Erikepaios. For more on Rhapsodies see West, 70.

[175] Less likely is the connection to the story of Euboulos of Messene who was captured by the Etruscans and taken to Etruria. Having recognized Euboulos as a follower of Pythagoras, Nausithoos defeated the pirates and delivered Euboulos to safety. Cf. Iamblichus, 57.

[176] Comparetti, D, "Laminetta Orfica di Cecilia Secundina," *Atene e Roma* 54-55 (1903): 161.

[177] Edmonds, 14.

latter tumulus, the dedication to Dionysus is firmly established. Invocation of Eukles/Eubouleus ties the soul to the divine child Dionysus, perhaps before he was killed. A1,4 then reads: "But Fate mastered me and the Thunderer, striking with his lightning."[178]

Anthropomorphism and Transformation

The soul is in a precarious position: it simultaneously recalls the death of Dionysus and pays homage to Zeus, who tried to destroy the Titans upon the eventual destruction of his child. A1, A2, and A3 tie in an important mythical event with the ascension and transformation of a mortal soul; the magical formulary are effectively used to merge past with present. Here we have a glimpse of a dual birth. First, the soul announces its mother as Persephone. Secondly, it acknowledges Dionysus' death by lightning. And thirdly, it affirms its re-birth from the bosom of the Pure Mistress or Queen of the Underworld. In a complex invocation, the soul simultaneously comes from and returns to the divine mother. Finally, the soul has escaped the wheel of fate, that force which has tied down many mortals to an existence of endless births. The one major difference between the three Timpone Piccolo lamellae is A1's inclusion of the "kid into milk" formula. That it has been compared to a Dionysian myth of birth and rebirth has been established in the other lamellae. An ancient rite contributed to the feeding of milk and honey to *mystes* in order to purify the soul prior to initiation; this use of milk as ritual

---

[178] Edmonds, 13. This is the nearly identical to line 5 in tablets A2 and A3, respectively.

was thought to originate in the Orphic and Dionysian mysteries.[179] Looking toward

certain traditions outside the Hellenic world may shed some light on this mysterious

practice. For instance, the Altai Tatars people from the Caucasus / Siberia region believe

that upon the birth of a child, the essence of life is brought from the Lake of Milk in

paradise by the god Yayutsi.[180] Line 10 shows not only that the soul has become

immortal in this intermediary stage, but has taken the form of a child or goat falling into

milk[181]:

> ὑριφος ἡς γάλ᾿ ηπετον[182]
> A kid I fell into milk.[183]

Further evidence of a fifth century B.C. theory of metempsychosis or

reincarnation has been shown through the writings of Pindar, the lyric poet from

Cynoscephalae in Boetia. Pindar's ancient grief formula of Persephone and the death of

Dionysos share similar elements with regard to the Pelinna tablets (P1/P2) from

---

[179] Apuleius of Madauros, *The Isis-Book* (Metamorphoses, Book XI), Ed. J. Gwyn Griffiths, Leiden: E. J. Brill: 1975.

[180] For more on this myth and its relation to the transmigration of souls and shamanistic practices of the Siberian traditions see Radlov, V.V, *Aus Sibirien: Lose Blatter aus Meinem Tagebuche.* Leipzig, T. D. Wigel: 1893.

[181] Aside from the A tablets, the "milk formula" only appears in P1 and P2 (Pelinna, Thessaly), where it is doubled up with the phrases "A bull you rushed into milk…A ram you fell into milk." It is significant, however, that anthropomorphic worship extends back into to Asia Minor, the Hittites and into the third millenium of Mesopotamia. Sacrifice of the bull shows itself in Minoan-Mycenaean cult practices and burial finds, and has been often associated with Dionysos. Other myths recount the transformation of Zeus as a bull in the abduction of Europa and the myth of Io. Cf. Burkert, 1998.

[182] A. Bernabe and A.I. Jimenez San Cristobal. *Instrucciones Para El Mas Alla: Las Laminillas Orficas de Oro.* (Madrid: Ediciones Clasicas, 2001) 270.

[183] Edmonds, 13.

Thessaly.[184] A similar connection with regard to solar theology in Pindar is evident in A4

from the Timpone Grande. In a fifth century B.C. *threnos* fragment from Pindar, the

doctrine of metempsychosis is all too clear:

ο῾σι δε Φερσεφὰνα ποιναν παλαιο πὴνθεος
δὴξεται, ἡς τὰν ῾περθεν ὠλιον κεινων ἠνῷτωι ὑτεϊ
ῷνδιδο ψυχῷς πῷλιν,
ἠκ ταν βασιλόες ῷγαυο
καὴ σθενει κραιπνο σοφαι τε μὴγιστοι
ὠνδρες α῾ξοντ᾽· ἡς τὰν λοιπὰν χρὰνον Ὥροες ῷ-
γνο— πρὰς ῷνθρῶπων καλὴονται

1. For those from whom Persephone exacts the penalty of
2. the ancient grief, in the ninth year she restores
3. their souls again to the sun above; from these
4. come august kings, and men who are swift in strength
5. and great in wisdom; for the rest of time by men
6. they are called saintly heroes.[185]

Time plays a crucial role in the transition of the soul, first upon its separation

from the material body through a period of judgement. What happens during this nine

year period is up for the reader to decide. Either the soul is resting before judgement or it

is fulfilling its journey in the underworld. In a striking parallel with A4, solar theology is

highlighted. Once the soul has been shown to be worthy of rebirth, Persephone "restores"

them to the sun above. While A4 begins with the soul departing from the light of the sun,

Pindar's *threnos* (Lines 2-3) attests to its final destination. Here, the soul is returning to

where it came from: the all-powerful god Helios. Mind and intelligence have survived

death too: Qualities of intelligence, wisdom, and strength help these souls to achieve the

mystic rite of immortality (Pindar, Line 5). As in the gold leaves, initiates must also keep

---

[184] Burkert, 1998.
[185] Pindar, "Carmina Cum Fragmentis, I-II," Trans. Snell, B., Maehler, H (Leipzig: Teubner, 1987-89) fr. 133.

sharp minds and exercise their wisdom in order to reach their destination. A4 warns that the initiate must keep a close eye on the environment, lest he picks the wrong path to walk on. Similarly, the patron Cecilia Secundina (A5) claims the gift of memory. Not only do the *mystai* have a clear mind, but "sharp minds" to address the guardians' questions (B10) beside the Lake of Memory. The final line "they are called saintly heroes" echoes the tablets which address the *mystai* as having entered the blessed ones (P1), the heroes (B1), the famed initiates and bacchics (B10), and the seats of the blessed (A2, A3). In terms of the oldest text to support a Greek theory (and practice) of metempsychosis, Walter Burkert's assessment of Pindar's second Olympian Ode is thus explained:

> According to Pindar there are three paths in the other world, three possibilities. Whoever has led a pious and just life finds a festive existence in the underworld, free from all cares in a place where the sun is shining at night; but evildoers suffer terrible things. The soul thereafter returns to the upper world where its fate is determined by its previous deeds; whoever stands the test three times enters the Island of the Blessed forever. One can compare with this the fact that in two of the Thurioi gold leaves immediate apotheosis is promised...[186]

With the fifth century B.C. having been agreed upon for the origin of the Thurii remains, their connection to a larger system of beliefs in reincarnation and immortality like those of the Derveni and Protogonos theogonies (Circa 500-400 B.C.) remains a possibility. Given the shorter forms of tablets A4 and C, they were transcribed from an earlier and more comprehensive manuscript like the Derveni Papyrus. The limitations on space provided by the lamellae, coupled with the cost of buying gold material, are obvious factors in considering what abbreviated versions would have been transcribed.

---

[186] Greek Religion, 299.

Chapter 5

Summary and Conclusions

The Orphic tablets represent a unique and sometimes perplexing look into ancient

ritual practices. The present study has shown that the gold leaves served to 1) function in

the afterlife (to protect the soul and ensure its immortalization), 2) provide mimetic

instructions to the soul upon bodily death, 3) act as a kind of "road-map" through the

underworld, 4) provide an account of the Orphic doctrine regarding purity of the soul, 5)

to document the role of deities in the afterlife, and 6) preserve the complex system of

passwords that the soul needs in order to complete immortalization.

There was an obvious taboo against forgetting one's past. Presumably, such a

taboo separated Orphic initiates who could remember past deeds (initiates who could

drink from the lake of memory) from those souls who forgot to follow the instructions on

the lamella. Pindar describes a third way for unholy souls and murderers who are

plunged into a pit of darkness:

ὑνθεν τ̊ν ὠπειρον ἠρεύγονται σκότον
βληχροὴ δνοφερῶς νυκτ̊ς ποταμοὴ

(Threnos 7: 15)

From there sluggish rivers of gloomy night
belch forth an endless darkness.[187]

Memory not only helped one remember past lives but prepared one to complete

the journey. One can only point to the numerous references within the lamellae that warn

against rebirth (A4, A5, P1, P2, B10 and B11). The gold lamellae support my hypothesis

---

[187] Pindar, "Nemean Odes, Isthmian Odes, Fragments," Trans. William H. Race
(Cambridge, Massachusetts: Harvard University Press, 1997) 366 & 367, respectively.

that a belief in reincarnation may have existed among these Orphic cults. In eight specific instances the soul announces its purity (A1, A2, A3, and A5), a common element that validates the soul's entrance among the blessed. Some explanations for the "pure" formula may be that the neophyte performed some kind of initiatory rite while still alive (perhaps through the auspices of a priestly cult that proclaimed authority in Orphic rituals). In this case the individual seeks to remind the guardians of his/her worthiness to enter among the prestigious ranks of Bacchoi and heroes. Seeing this in another light, we turn again to the Orphic belief in Persephone or the "Queen" who lies below the Earth. The fact that the soul announces his/her own purity in the same sentence as Persephone is not happenstance. For instance, we have already established that Persephone was, in some respects, worshipped in the same vein as her mother Demeter or Rhea. Being "pure" may indicate that one is naturally pure since he/she was born from Persephone and is now returning to her in the afterlife. Hence the invocation, "I am the daughter (B6) or son (B7, B8) of Earth and starry Heaven."

The other implication of leaves is the Orphic differentiation between unholy (profane) and pious souls. The former are preoccupied with feelings of guilt (the death of Dionysus, the abduction of Persephone). The latter type of individual has remembered past events, actions and habits but has exceeded beyond this lower state by becoming pure. It is as if the lamella has freed the individual, providing them with a token to gain immortality.

With the exception of the bone plates from Olbia, all of the lamellae were made from gold. Gold would ensure its preservation for years to come, and prevent its deterioration even as the body decomposed. While it was probably expensive to commission such an item for one's burial, its durability clearly outweighed such materials as wood, lead or even leather. Whether in Pharsalos, Thessaly, or in Hipponion (south Italy), the importance of gold remained an important aspect of immortality among these Orphic followers. It was important enough to be placed with the human remains and was powerful enough to transmit the written formulas into the underworld. Furthermore, these Orphics may have believed that a lamella would transcend beyond the material and into metaphysical space. It certainly did have power, both in its material nature (gold) and in the precious (secretive) written formulary of Orpheus. Certainly we cannot expect all of these objects to have been placed after the burial of such individuals. Take for instance the lamella from Petelia, it was housed in a cylinder with a chain that was to be worn as a necklace. This is a perfect example of a functional object whose purpose was aesthetic, hence its classification as jewelry in the British Museum. The Petelia owner may have worn it in everyday life as a protective amulet, so as to remind him/herself (and the deities) of the afterlife. These lamellae, therefore, served a protective function in the lives of these believers. A Chaldaean inscription on a tomb of Sardanapallus tells of an Assyrian named Ninos who turns to ash because he lacked the appropriate token. Ninos recognizes his fate by stating:

ἦγ᾽ δ᾽ ἦς ἰΑιδην ο᾽τε χρυσ᾽ν ο᾽θ᾽ ἦππον

(Phoenix 1: 20)

And I to Hades neither gold did bring.[188]

---

[188] Theophrastus, "Characters," Trans. J. M. Edmonds (Cambridge, Massachusetts: Harvard University Press, 1946) 244-245.

Ninos forgets to bring an important item during his underworld journey, that of carrying gold. The precious material serves as a gift to the gods, a ritual reminder of one's allegiance to these powers. The lamellae also confirm the ancient belief in the separation of the body from the soul. Body, then, becomes identified with a coffin or prison, while the soul is the thing or essence that is trapped within. The soul must get out but is trapped in the wheel of life and suffers a number of rebirths because it has not remembered its past deeds. Forgetfulness, the antithesis of memory, stifles the soul from getting at truth and realizing its own potential toward greatness. The golden leaves provide the soul with an opportunity to ascend, as it were, among the ranks of the blessed. We can break these concepts down into the following:

Body = Prison   (Present time)

Soul = Knowledge   (Received knowledge in past)

Soul + Body = Confusion

Soul – Body = Truth / Knowledge

Death was not only seen in terms of a future event but a past event imposed on immortals like Dionysus and Orpheus. This momentous act of severing the godhead into several parts persuaded individuals in believing in their own immortality. The child of Zeus was a powerful presence who overcame the restraints of death and became immortal; the initiate identified with the murder of Dionysus as a self-inflicting punishment that was equated with redemption and enlightenment. One is reminded of Athena who preserves the heart (equivalent to the divine soul) of Dionysus by interring it with mock gypsum (analogous to the body).[189] Was the initiate re-enacting the death of Dionysus in order to claim immortality? Did the initiate believe that Persephone was the first mother, the father being Zeus? I believe this to be a strong possibility, since in the tablet from Pherai, Thessaly, the initiate is addressed as the "Male child of the thyrsos,"[190] the child of Persephone.

The gold leaves afford us the opportunity of understanding how some ancients viewed the afterlife. Orphics were not only concerned with the destination of the soul but with controlling the process of separating the soul from the body. It was not good enough to believe that one could recite a prayer in the afterlife; one had to remember his/her past life. Furthermore, it was expected that the soul carry the tablet in the underworld and remember to follow the directions. The directions in the tablets provide a clear path for the soul to navigate in the realm of the deceased; as if knowing the temptations that awaited the soul, it must be specific. A temptation that the soul must avoid is drinking from the lake of Lethe or Forgetfulness. The soul is warned that the "glowing white cypress tree" is near, and it is tempting for the thirsty soul to drink from. Perhaps the cypress tree, in all its splendor and beauty, was so dangerous that any soul would be distracted, believing that it led one to immortality. That was not the path for the soul to travel.

We know, for example, that such "Orphic" cults became tolerant in worshipping a number of deities. The numerous references in the lamellae provide a "who's-who" in ancient mythology: Zeus is invoked as the "Thunderer" (A1, A2, A3) or "Radiant one"

---

[189] Proclus, Hymni. Accedunt Hymnorum Fragmenta, Epigrammata, Scholia, Fontium et Locorum Similium Apparatus, Indices. Trans. and Ed. Ernst Vogt. (Wiesbaden: In Kommission bei O. Harrassowitz, 1957) 35, 210, 214.

[190] Edmonds, 18.

(A5). With respect to the "Earth and Starry" heaven formula (B1-B11), is the former symbolic for Zeus and the latter Persephone? The Derveni Papyrus (PDERV) provides us with more information about the Orphic doctrine than any document in papyrology. The contents of PDERV reveal a complex history of man's origins. In order to present a cohesive theory regarding Orphic theology, I have broken down the various passages in PDERV to present the following lineage:

1. Night –

2. Sun (*Aidoion*) / Earth – Kronos – Zeus (*Ocean, Air*)

3. Persuasion / Harmony / Aphrodite

4. Earth = Mother = Rhea = Hera = Gaia = Demeter = Hestia = Meter = Deio[191]

Empedocles

   Reincarnation was a belief among some "Orphics," and it formed the center of their teaching from the fifth century B.C. until the second century A.D. Evidence for this is preserved by the invention of the gold leaves, its contents protected by the multiple folds that functioned to be unwrapped by the soul. Lamella A4,1 (Thurii, Timpone Grande (4th B.C.) illustrates this Greek doctrine of metempsychosis: The soul departs the light of the sun (Helios or father Zeus) in order to be re-united with mother Persephone in the sacred meadows (achieving immortality). We are reminded of the philosopher Empedocles who writes of "meadows" as female genitals. Citing fr. 66 of Empedocles':

---

[191] Andre Laks & Glenn W. Most "A Provisional Translation of the Derveni Papyrus". In: *Studies on the Derveni Papyrus*. (Oxford: Clarendon Press, 1997) 10-22.

meadows is "λειμ῁νας,"[192] with "λειμ῁νάς" appearing in A4,6 and "λειμ῁να" in

Ph,2.[193] In fr. 137, Empedocles speaks directly about the soul reincarnating into an

animal: "μορφὲν . . . ὦλλάξαντα."[194] This teaching is consistent with his beliefs

regarding the separation of impure and pure souls in the afterlife. We would be remiss if

we ignored the various traditions, stories, and legends that have been attributed to the

philosopher Empedocles (477 B.C. – 432 B.C.). In certain respects he can fall in and out

of this philosopher category by entertaining stories of magic and necromancy.

Empedocles is a man of superhuman powers (Empedocles 8: 54),[195] a self-proclaimed

immortal (Empedocles 8: 54) and diviner who kept a woman in suspended death for

thirty days while she never breathed (Empedocles 8: 61-62).[196] More than a physician,

the so-named philosopher is said to have cured Panthea, a woman from Agrigentum,

Sicily (Empedocles 8: 69). It was for this reason that he begins to offer a sacrifice, and as

he climbs Mount Etna, plunges himself into the fiery crater (Empedocles 8: 69).[197] This

is the most fantastic story we have of Empedocles, and one that has caused doubt among

historians and writers for centuries. Is Empedocles asserting his immortality by plunging

---

[192] Empedocles, Περὴ "Φύσεως and Καθαρμοί," Trans. Henry W. Johnstone, Jr. (Bryn Mawr, PA: Bryn Mawr Commentaries, 1985) 30. Empedocles who lived between 477 and 432 B.C., is known to have taught a doctrine of metempsychosis that is closely aligned to that of Pythagoras. His work during this period therefore confirms that teachings of reincarnation / metempsychosis were circulating in southern Sicily and in the motherland of Greece.

[193] Edmonds, 3 and 12 respectively.

[194] Empedocles, 43.

[195] Diogenes Laertius, "Lives of the Eminent Philosophers," Trans. R.D. Hicks (Cambridge, Massachusetts: Harvard University Press, 2000) 371.

[196] Diogenes Laertius, "Lives of the Eminent Philosophers," Trans. R.D. Hicks (Cambridge, Massachusetts: Harvard University Press, 2000) 377.

[197] Diogenes Laertius, "Lives of the Eminent Philosophers," Trans. R.D. Hicks (Cambridge, Massachusetts: Harvard University Press, 2000) 383.

into the volcanic crater or is it a simple sacrifice? Mount Etna has often been considered

to be a sacred place among the ancients, serving both Chthonic and Olympian traditions.

The subterranean channels and rivers of fire act as portals or entrances to Tartarus[198] and

the heavenly realms (Phaedo : 111d-112a). Empedocles returns to fire, cleansing his

body as he is submerged in lava. The story ends by suggesting that he has disappeared,

vanished into nothing, and has left the Earth by mysterious circumstances. The symbolic,

mythological and religious explanations are profound in that they raise Empedocles to an

immortal standing. He has defeated death, used his powers to heal others of their

misfortunes, and took the initiative in transforming his self from mortal to spirit. There is

still the question of how Empedocles could have been incinerated in flame if his tomb

existed in Megara.[199] In transcending the physics of everyday life, his assertion to

immortality is substantiated by the return of his body. Part of the legend even asserts that

after he had fallen into the crater of Mount Etna, one of his bronze slippers had

miraculously jumped up from the flames intact (Empedocles 8: 69-70).[200] Symbolic in

structure, these events point to the endurance of the spirit, the destruction of the body,

and the inconsequential nature of material possessions. As if saying "hey look at me, I

am now in another place, go ahead and take my bronze slipper," Empedocles' storytellers

appear to be poking fun at the idea of mortality and apotheosis. Does the soul return to /

from the sun in the same way that Empedocles fell into the volcanic fire of Mount Etna?

In Olympian 2, Pindar recounts how the transmigration of souls serves the blessed and

---

[198] Plato, "Phaedo," 111d-112a.
[199] Diogenes Laertius, "Lives of the Eminent Philosophers," Trans. R.D. Hicks (Cambridge, Massachusetts: Harvard University Press, 2000) 389.
[200] Diogenes Laertius, "Lives of the Eminent Philosophers," Trans. R.D. Hicks (Cambridge, Massachusetts: Harvard University Press, 2000) 385.

profane. Semele endures a death by Zeus' lightning and ends up living with the

Olympians (Olympian 2: 25), while Ino who leapt into the sea is granted an immortal

existence (Olympian 2: 29). Pindar speaks of forgetfulness as a way to alleviate the pain

that often plagues the mortal life. Time (Kronos) cannot undo these events (Olympian 2:

17), for he has no domain over what Fate and Destiny decree as law. The allusion of one

leaping into one of the elements (fire, air, earth, or water) represents an end to one's

mortality, for it is in praise of immortality that one is released from these bonds.

Empedocles immerses himself into volcanic fire, while Ino drowns herself in water, and

Semele is consumed by lightning. The clearest example of transmigration and

metempsychosis is found in the example of souls who have lived three times in Hades

and on earth. Pious souls are described by Pindar as courageous individuals, having been

sent to the Isle of the Blessed, and travelling the road of Zeus to the "tower of Kronos

(Olympian 2: 70-75)."[201]

Materialism and Orphic Theology

If the soul had nothing to fear, then why carry these gold tablets to the grave? Did

the magoi believe such an amulet would protect him from the horrors of Hades, or more

specifically, from being re-born into the form of an animal, plant or human? If the

Orphics did not believe in the reincarnation, then why did the soul need to become

immortal? We cannot forget that materialism played an important role in Orphic

theology; the lamellae were exclusively made of golden sheets, aside from the bones

---

[201] Pindar, "Olympian Odes and Pythian Odes I," ed. and Trans. William H. Race
(Cambridge, Massachusetts: Harvard University Press, 1997) 71.

from Olbia. We do not know if wooden tablets were in use at the time, or if leather was one of the materials. The importance placed in gold, a precious metal, was undeniable. They believed it to last for centuries, to retain its color, and most importantly, to help transport the symbolic language across the spiritual barrier. If the soul was not buried with gold lamella, did it merely die off with the body? What would happen to souls who carried the lamella but took the wrong turn? Why didn't the Orphics use lead or other less expensive materials like bronze? The latin term for Defixiones or katadesmoi in Greek (Lead curse tablets), differ greatly from their golden counterparts since they deal with necromancy and control over demonic spirits. Lead tablets are used as amulets, aggressive objects in black magic, or in the formal sense of the word, magical praxis. The lead tablet from Fayum (100-200 A.D.) is folded vertically and then folded from top to bottom to form a pocket. In it, Alexandros commands the demon to enter into conversation with him.[202] Lead tablets appear to distinguish between the soul and demon, making them separate entities. In the gold tablets, divinities are revered, and prayed to for immortality, while the lead tablets command deities and demons to do their bidding in the mortal realm (wishes and spells to be granted). We notice sparse references to Egyptian divinities like the god Kneph, creator and originator who is the wind or spirit of life. Another reference to Hermes or Thoth illustrates the importance of writing, magical glyphs and wisdom. Thoth is the lord of wisdom and magic, the writer of many sacred books who ushers forth writing and knowledge among men and immortals. Other lead tablets provide further instructions, instructing the magus to write magical inscriptions on a laurel leaf so that it may be placed under the head during sleep. As far as we know,

---

[202] Daniel, R. W. and Maltomini, F, "Supplementum Magicum: Vol. II," (Koln: West Deutscher Verlag, 1992) 76-77.

these lead tablets deal with curing illnesses, reversing bad luck, placing a curse on an enemy, and requesting dreams.[203]

If these Orphics did not believe in metempsychosis, then why place such a heavy emphasis on purity? As one can see, the study of this subject raises many questions. We know that the Orphic cults were much more complex than has previously been thought. The uninscribed lamellae[204] from Sfakaki, Crete (Sfakaki, Rethymno Museum, Inv. # Μ[ετάλλινα] 897, Μ[ετάλλινα] 2887, and Μ[ετάλλινα] 964) are most intriguing. They lack the written formulas, passwords, instruction, and invocations that serve to guide the soul. Two out of the three contain hatch-like patterning, with lamella Μ[ετάλλινα] 897 containing thin crossing lines and Μ[ετάλλινα] 964 having a chess-like pattern that covers the entire lamella. At some point in history, these symbols and patterns became lost to the world. The significance that uninscribe lamellae were found with inscribed lamellae show that they functioned in similar funeral contexts. Alas, with the protective power of a lamaella, the soul avoids reincarnation: carrying such a token becomes the primary motivation of the initiate, and a gold lamella serves as a magical tool in this effort. Initiates into the mysteries chose to accept and follow Orpheus' teachings precisely because he cheated death. He entered Hades, survived its dangers and survived dismemberment. The gold lamellae provide this kind of access to a higher existence, one that unlocks the secret by promising a release of the soul from the body.

---

[203] Daniel, R. W. and Maltomini, F, "Supplementum Magicum: Vol. II," (Koln: West Deutscher Verlag, 1992) 133, 177-178.

[204] Tzifopoulos, Yannis Z. *The Dionysiac(-Orphic) Lamellae of Crete*: With Contributions on the Archaeological Context by Irene Gavrilaki, Stella Kalogeraki, Eyrydiki Kefalidou, Popi Galanaki and Giorgos Rethemiotakis. (Unpublished manuscript given to me by Professor Yannis Z. Tzifopoulos, University of Crete, 2003) 21-22.

Appendix I

Glossary of Terms

ἀκροαταί: priests trained by Musaios and followers

Agyrtai, Chrêsmôdiai: Priests of an Orphic cult.

Amystēriastos: people who are uninitiated into the mysteries.

Anamnesis: Plato's version of the lake of memory (Mnemosyne). The sacred water that Transforms the soul into an immortal.

Bacchoi: (βάχχοι) the pious souls who achieve immortality and enter the ranks of the

holy. (see tablets B10, 16).

Chthonic deities: (chthonios) gods of the earth, a distinct part of the Greek pantheon Separate from the Olympian or heavenly gods. Chthonios deities included Demeter, Hermes, Zeus, Hecate, Hades/Pluton, and Persephone.

Epistomion: an object that blocks a hole or gap; a golden lamella in the shape of a mouth.

Formularies: formulas used in the mystery traditions to invoke a deity. The act of Reciting or writing a formula in order to expect an outcome. Also may have formed parts of a larger hymn or song written by Orpheus.

Gnōsis: Knowledge, often referring to the secrets held by the mystery traditions.

Lake of Lethe: refers to forgetfulness. If a soul drinks from this it cannot remember its past lives.

Lake of Mnemosyne: the final destination in Hades where the soul must drink from. Mnemosyne also refers to the mother of the nine muses.

Magus / Magoi / Mystai: priests, teachers, educators or advisers of theogonies. Specialists
In rites, sacrifices, texts, astrology, and sorcery.

Orpheotelestês: Orphic priests who publicly practiced the mysteries.

Orphikoi: priests who remained in secret groups.

Peithein Theous: to act of invoking a deity, an invocation written down or read out loud.

Teletai: priests trained by Orpheus

Appendix II

Gold tablets[205]

Siglum	Location	Date
A1	Thurii, Timpone Piccolo	4th B.C.
A2	Thurii, Timpone Piccolo	4th B.C.
A3	Thurii, Timpone Piccolo	4th B.C.
A4	Thurii, Timpone Grande	4th B.C.
A5	Rome	260 A.D.
C	Thurii, Timpone Grande	4th B.C.
P1	Pelinna, Thessaly	end of 4th B.C.
P2	Pelinna, Thessaly	end of 4th B.C.
B1	Petelia, Italy	4th B.C.
B2	Pharsalos, Thessaly	350-320 B.C.
B3	Eleutherna, Crete	2nd B.C.
B4	Eleutherna, Crete	2nd B.C.
B5	Eleutherna, Crete	2nd B.C.
B6	Mylopetra, Crete	2nd B.C.
B7	Eleutherna, Crete	2nd B.C.
B8	Eleutherna, Crete	2nd B.C.
B9	Thessaly	4th B.C.
B10	Hipponion, Italy	end of 5th B.C.
B11	central Sicily	3rd B.C.
Ph	Pherai, Thessaly	??
El	Eleutherna, Crete	2nd B.C.

Uninscribed gold tablets[206]

Siglum	Location	Date
Sr1	Sfakaki, Crete	1st A.D.
Sr2	Sfakaki, Crete	1st A.D.
Sr3	Sfakaki, Crete	1st A.D

Illustrations

---

[205] Edmonds, R. "*Roads Not Taken: Explorations of the 'Orphic' Gold Tablets*," Unpublished transcript from the Chicago Humanities Institute (University of Chicago, 1997) 19.

[206] Tzifopoulos, Yannis Z. *The Dionysiac(-Orphic) Lamellae of Crete*: With Contributions on the Archaeological Context by Irene Gavrilaki, Stella Kalogeraki, Eyrydiki Kefalidou, Popi Galanaki and Giorgos Rethemiotakis. (Unpublished manuscript given to me by Professor Yannis Z. Tzifopoulos, University of Crete, 2003) 21-22.

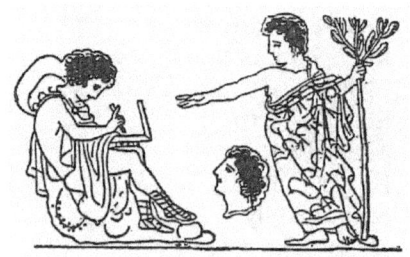

Fig.1. Red-figure kylix representing Orpheus. Fitzwilliam Museum (Inventory number not published). From Jane Ellen Harrison, <u>Prolegomena to the Study of Greek Religion</u>.

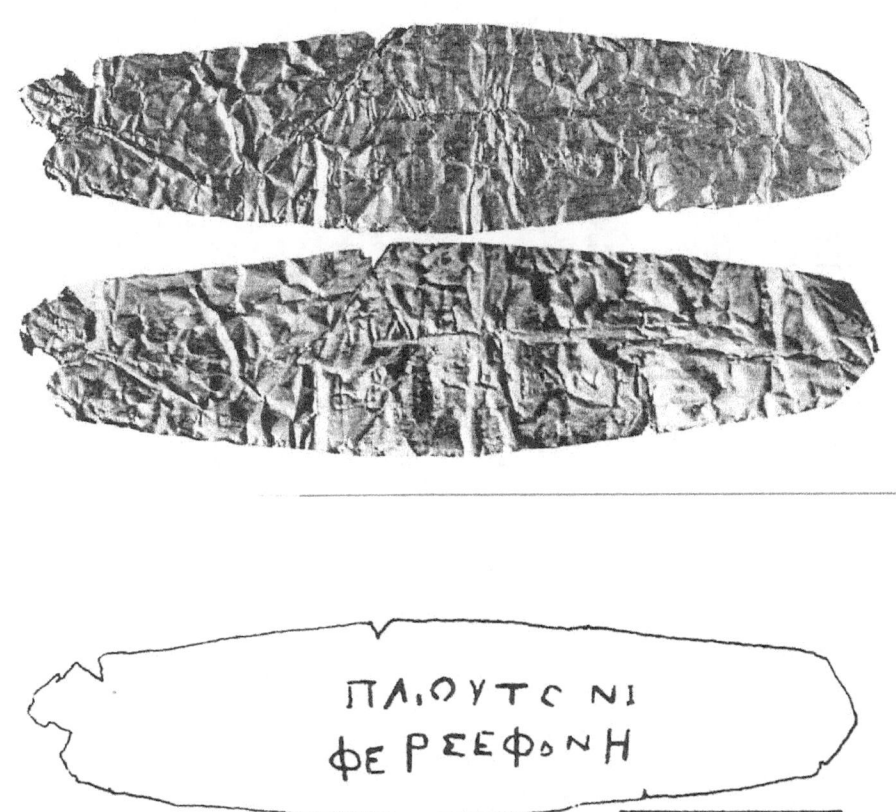

Fig. 2. Gold epistomion. 25 B.C. –40 A.D., Rethymno Museum (Inventory number: M 896), H. 0.012 (left)-0.018 (center), W. 0.075, Th. Less than 0.001, L.H. 0.002-0.004, Weight: 0,4 gr. From Irini Gavrilaki and Yannis Z. Tsifopoulos, "An 'Orphic-Dionysiac' Gold Epistomion from Sfakaki near Rethymno."

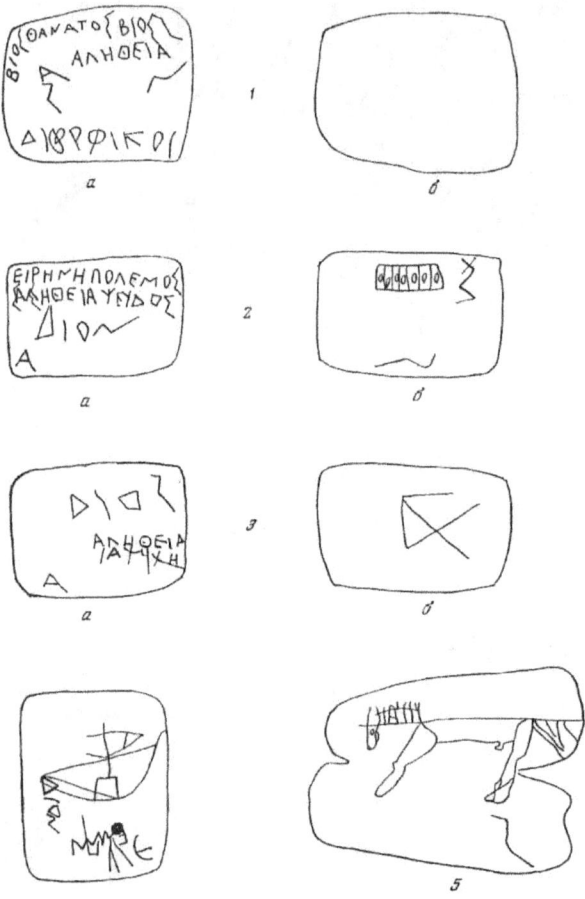

Fig. 3. Bone plates from Olbia. Fifth century BC. Institute of Archaeology of the Ukrainian Academy of Sciences (Inventory number: O-51/3695). From A.S. Rusiaeva, "Orfizm I Kul't Dionisa v Ol'vii." 2001.

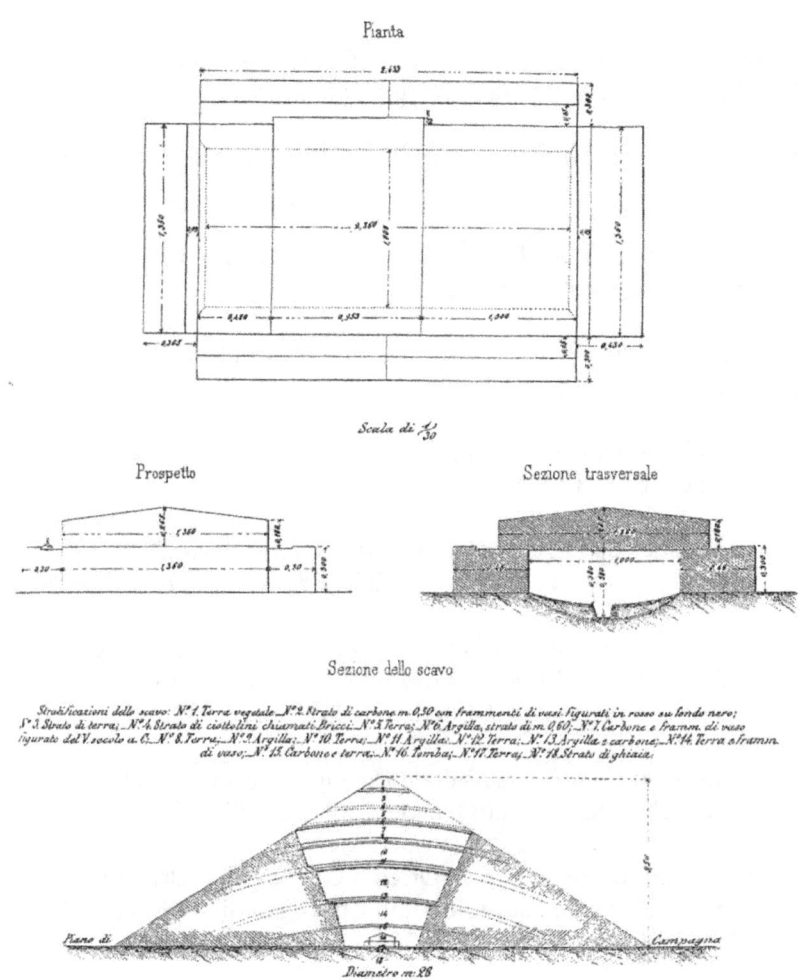

Fig. 4. Drawing of the Timpone Grande at Thurii according to Cavallari. From Cavallari, F.S. Notizie degli Scavi di Antichita. 1879.

Bibliography

I.   Works Cited

Abel, Eugenius. *Acc. Procli Hymni, Hymni magici, Hymnus in Isim aliaque eiusmodi carmina*. Hildesheim, Gerstenberg, 1971.

Aelian. *Historical Miscellany (Varia Histirica)*. Trans. N. G. Wilson. Cambridge, Massachusetts: Harvard University Press, 1997.

Alderink, L.J. *Creation and Salvation in Ancient Orphism*. Ann Arbor: Scholars Press, 1981.

Anonymous. *Select Papyri: Vol. III*. Trans. D. L. Page. Cambridge, Massachusetts: Harvard University Press, 1970.

Apuleius of Madauros, *The Isis-Book:* Metamorphoses, Book XI. Ed. J. Gwyn Griffiths, Leiden: E. J. Brill: 1975.

Belin de Ballu, E. *Olbia; Cité Antique du Littoral Nord de la Mer Noire*. Leiden, E. J. Brill, 1972.

Bernabe, A. and Jimenez San Cristobal, A.I. *Instrucciones Para El Mas Alla: Las Laminillas Orficas de Oro*. Madrid: Ediciones Clasicas, 2001.

Betz, H.D. "The Formation of Authoritative Tradition in the Greek Magical Papyri." *Jewish and Christian Self-Definition: Volume Three, Self-Definition in the Graeco-Roman World.* London: SCM Press, 1982.

Burkert, Walter. *Lore and Science in Ancient Pythagoreanism,.* Cambridge, Massachusetts: Harvard University Press, 1972.

Burkert, Walter. "Le Laminette auree: da Orfeo a Lampone" in Orfismo in Magna Grecia: Atti del quattordicesimo Convegno di Studi sulla Magna Grecia. Arte Tipografica: Napoli, 1975.

Burkert, Walter. "Orphism and Bacchic Mysteries: New Evidence and Old Problems of Interpretation." *Protocol of the 28th Colloquy of the Center for Hermeneutical Studies in Hellenistic and Modern Culture.* Berkeley: Center for Hermeneutical Studies, 1977.

Burkert, Walter. *Greek Religion*. Cambridge, Massachusetts: Harvard University Press, 1998.

Burn, A.R. *The Penguin History of Greece*. London: Penguin Books, 1985.

Cavallari, F. S. *Notizie degli Scavi di Antichita*. Rome: Accademia Nazionale dei Lincei, 1879.

Clement of Alexandria, *Extracts from the Writings of Clement of Alexandria*. New York: John Lane, 1905.

Clement of Alexandria. *Exhortation to the Greeks and The Rich Man's Salvation to the Newly Baptized*. Trans. G.W. Butterworth. Ed. G.P. Goold. Cambridge, Massachusetts: Harvard University Press, 1999.

Comparetti, D. "Laminetta Orfica di Cecilia Secundina," *Atene e Roma* 54-55 (1903): 161.

Comparetti, D. "Sibari," *Notizie degli Scavi* 3 (1879): 156.

Demosthenes, *Orations XXI-XXVI*. Trans. J. H. Vince. Cambridge, Massachusetts: Harvard University Press, 1998.

Diels, H. and W. Kranz, *Die Fragmente der Vorsokratiker* (in three volumes), 6th edition. Dublin and Zürich: Weidmann, 1952.

Diodorus of Sicily. *I: Books I and II, 1-34*. Trans. C. H. Oldfather. Cambridge, Massachusetts: Harvard University Press, 1933.

Diodorus of Sicily. Book II. Trans. C. H. Oldfather. Cambridge, Massachusetts: Harvard University Press, 1933.

Edmonds, R. *Roads Not Taken: Explorations of the 'Orphic' Gold Tablets*. Unpublished transcript from the Chicago Humanities Institute, University of Chicago, 1997.

Empedocles. *The Extant Fragments*. Trans. & Ed. M. R. Wright. London: Bristol Classical Press, 1995.

Empedocles. Φύσεως and Καθαρμο–. Trans. Henry W. Johnstone, Jr. Bryn Mawr, PA: Bryn Mawr Commentaries, 1985.

Eratosthenes. *Eratosthenis Catasterismorum Reliquiae : Accedunt Prologomena et Epimetra Tria*. Trans. Carolus Robert. Berolini : Apud Weidmannos, 1963.

Euripides. *Select Papyri: Vol. III*. Trans. D. L. Page. Cambridge, Massachusetts: Harvard University Press, 1970.

Fontenrose, Joseph. *The Delphic Oracle*: *Its Responses and Operations*. Berkeley: University of California Press, 1978.

Franz, G. *Bulletino dell' Instituto di Corr. Arch, 1836.*

Gavrilaki, I. and Tsifopoulos, Y. Z. "An 'Orphic-Dionysiac' Gold Epistomion from Sfakaki near Rethymno." *BCH* 122 (1998): 346.

Giangrande, G. "La lamina orfica di Hipponion" in Agostino Masaracchia., ed., *Orfeo e l'orfismo: Atti del Seminario Nazionale.* Roma: Gruppo Editoriale Internazionale, 1993.

Guarducci, M. *Inscriptiones creticae, Opera et Consilio Friderici Halbherr Collectae.* Rome: Libreria dello Stato, 1939.

Guthrie, W. K. C. *Orpheus and Greek Religion*. New York: W.W. Norton & Company, Inc, 1966.

Harrison, Jane Ellen. *Prolegomena to the Study of Greek Religion.* New York: Arno Press, 1975.

Harrison, Jane Ellen. *Themis: A Study of the Social Origins of Greek Religion.* London: Merlin Press, 1963.

Heraclitus, *Fragments*. Trans. Brooks Haxton. London: Penguin Classics, 2001.

Herodotus. *Books III-IV.* Trans. A. D. Godley. Cambridge, Massachusetts: Harvard University Press, 2000.

Herodotus. *Books I-II.* Trans. A. D. Godley. Cambridge, Massachusetts: Harvard University Press, 1996.

Herodotus. *Book IV.* Trans. R.W. Macan. New York: Arno Press, 1973.

Hesiod. *Theogony and Works and Days.* Trans. M.L. West. Oxford: Oxford University Press, 1988.

Huffman, C. A., *Philolaus of Croton: Pythagorean and Presocratic*. Cambridge: Cambridge University Press, 1993.

Iacobacci, G. "La laminetta Aurea di Hipponion: Osservazioni Dialettologiche" in Agostino Masaracchia., ed., *Orfeo e l'orfismo: Atti del Seminario Nazionale.* Roma: Gruppo Editoriale Internazionale, 1993.

Iamblichus. *On the Pythagorean Life*. Trans. Gillian Clark. Liverpool: Liverpool University Press, 1989.

Iamblichus of Chalcis, *De Mysteriis Aegyptiorum,* Ed. Stephen Ronan, Trans. Thomas Taylor & Alexander Wilder. Hastings, E. Sussex, England: Chthonios Books: 1989.

Joubin, A. *Inscription Cretoise Relative a l' Orphisme.* BCH, 17, 1893.

Julian. *The Works of the Emperor Julian: Vol. II.* Trans. Wilmer Cave Wright. Cambridge, Massachusetts: Harvard University Press, 1969.

Julian. *The Works of the Emperor Julian: Vol. III.* Trans. Wilmer Cave Wright. Cambridge, Massachusetts: Harvard University Press, 1953.

Kahn, Charles H. *Pythagoras and the Pythagoreans.* Indianapolis/Cambridge: Hackett Publishing Company, Inc, 2001.

Kerényi, K. *Dionysos : Urbild des unzerstörbaren Lebens.* Munich: Langen Mueller, 1976.

Kern, O. *Orphicorum Fragmenta.* Berolini: Apud Weidmannos, 1922.

King, Leonard W. *Babylonian Magic and Sorcery: Being The Prayers of the Lifting of the Hand.* London: Luzac and Co., 1896.

Kirk, G.S. *Heraclitus: The Cosmic Fragments.* Cambridge: University Press, 1970.

Kirk,G.S. Raven, J.E. and Schofield, M. *The Presocratic Philosophers: Second Edition.* Cambridge: Cambridge University Press, 1983.

Karasev, A.N. "Diary of archeological excavations in Olbia in 1951." *In Report of the Olbia expedition for 1951.* Moscow: Archive of the Institute of Archeology of the Academy of Sciences of the Ukrainian Soviet Socialist Republic, 1951.

Kurtz., Donna C. and Boardman, John. *Greek Burial Customs.* London: Thames and Hudson, 1971.

Laertius, Diogenes. Lives of Eminent Philosophers. Trans. R. D. Hicks, Massachusetts: Harvard University Press, 1965.

Laks, A. and Most, G. W. "A Provisional Translation of the Derveni Papyrus". In: *Studies on the Derveni Papyrus.* Oxford: Clarendon Press, 1997.

Lexicon Iconographicum Mythologiae Classicae: VII. Zurich: ArtemisVerlag, 1994.

Linforth, M. *The Arts of Orpheus.* Berkeley: University of California Press, 1941.

Luck, George. *Arcana Mundi.* Baltimore: The Johns Hopkins University Press, 1985.

Marshall, F.H., M.A., *Catalogue of the Jewellery, Greek, Etruscan, and Roman, In the Departments of Antiquities, British Museum.* London: Printed by order of the Trustees, 1911.

Nock, A.D. *Essays on Religion and the Ancient World. Oxford: Clarendon Press, 1972.*

Pindar. *The Odes and Selected Fragments.* London: J.M. Dent, 1997.

Pindar. *Olympian Odes and Pythian Odes I.* Ed. and Trans. William H. Race. Cambridge, Massachusetts: Harvard University Press, 1997.

Pindar. *Carmina Cum Fragmentis, I-II*, Trans. Snell, B., Maehler, H. Leipzig: Teubner, 1987-89.

Plato. *Euthyphro, Apology, Crito, Phaedo, Phaedrus.* Trans. Harold North Fowler. Ed. Jeffrey Henderson. Cambridge, Massachusetts: Harvard University Press, 2001.

Plato. *The Republic: Books VI-X.* Trans. Paul Shorey. Cambridge, Massachusetts: Harvard University Press, 2000.

Plato. *The Republic: Books I-V.* Trans. Paul Shorey. Cambridge, Massachusetts: Harvard University Press, 1999.

Plato. *Symposium and Phaedrus*, New York: Dover, 1993.

Pliny, *Natural History XXV*, Trans. W.H.S. Jones. Cambridge, Massachusetts: Harvard University Press, 2001.

Natural History XX-XXIII, Trans. W.H.S. Jones. Cambridge, Massachusetts: Harvard University Press, 1999.

Natural History III-VII, Trans. H. Rackham. Cambridge, Massachusetts: Harvard University Press, 1999.

Plotinus, *Select Works of Plotinus.* Ed. G.R.S. Meade, Trans. Thomas Taylor. London: G. Bell and Sons, Ltd., 1941.

Proclus. Hymni. Accedunt Hymnorum Fragmenta, Epigrammata, Scholia, Fontium et Locorum Similium Apparatus, Indices. Trans. and Ed. Ernst Vogt. Wiesbaden, In Kommission bei O. Harrassowitz, 1957.

Pugliese, C. G. "Un Sepolcro di Hipponion e un Nuovo Testo Orfico", Parola del Passato 29, 1974.

Radlov, V.V. *Aus Sibirien: Lose Blatter aus Meinem Tagebuche.* Leipzig, T. D. Wigel: 1893.

Rhodius, Apollonius. The Argonautica. Trans. R. C. Seaton. Cambridge, Massachusetts: Harvard University Press, 1967.

Riedweg, C. "Initiation Tod Unterwelt: Beobachtungen zur Kommunikationssituation und narrativen Technik der Orphisch-Bakschischen Goldblattchen" in *Ansichten Griechischer Rituale: Geburtstags-Symposium fur Walter Burkert.* Stuttgart: B.G. Teubner, 1998.

Rusiaeva, A.S. "Orfizm I Kul't Dionisa v Ol'vii", *Vestnik Drevney Istorii* Vol. 1, 1978.

Smith, C. and Comparetti, D. "The Petelia Gold Tablet." *The Journal of Hellenic Studies* Vol 3, 1882.

Tinnefeld, F. "Referat Uber Zwei Russische Aufsatze." *Zeitschrift Fur Papyrologie und Epigraphik* Vol. 38, 1980.

Tsantsanoglou, K. and Parassoglou, G. M. *Two Gold Lamellae from Thessaly.* *ΕΛΛHNIKA*, 38, 1987.

Tzifopoulos, Yannis Z. *The Dionysiac(-Orphic) Lamellae of Crete*: With Contributions on the Archaeological Context by Irene Gavrilaki, Stella Kalogeraki, Eyrydiki Kefalidou, Popi Galanaki and Giorgos Rethemiotakis. (Unpublished manuscript given to me by Professor Yannis Z. Tzifopoulos, University of Crete, 2003).

Verdelis, N.M. Χαλκό τεφροδὸχος κάλπις ὰκ Φαρσάλων, in 'Αρχ., 1950-1951.

Watkins, Calvert. *How to Kill a Dragon.* Oxford: Oxford University Press, 1995.

Wasowicz, A. *Olbia Pontique et Son Territoire : L'Aménagement de L'espace.* Paris: Belles-lettres, 1975.

West, M.L. "The Orphics of Olbia." *Zeitschrift Fur Papyrologie und Epigraphik* Vol. 45, 1982.

West, M.L. *The Orphic Poems.* Oxford: Clarendon Press, 1983.

Xenocrates, *Frammenti / Senocrate, Ermodoro*, ed. and trans. by Margherita Isnardi Parente. Napoli : Bibliopolis, 1982.

Zuntz, G. *Persephone: Three Essays on Religion and Thought in Magna Graecia.* Oxford: Clarendon Press., 1971.

II. Works Consulted

Euripides. *Bacchae.* Ed. E.R. Dodds. Oxford: Clarendon Press, 1986.

Guthrie, W.K.C. *The Greeks and Their Gods.* Boston: Beacon Press, 1950.

Irwin, Eleanor. "The Orpheus of Virgil and Ovid: *flebile nescio quid.*" *Orpheus: The Metamorphoses of a Myth.* Ed. John Warden. Toronto: University of Toronto Press, 1982.

Otto, Walter F. *Dionyus: Myth and Cult.* Indianapolis: Indiana University Press, 1965.

III. Works to Be Consulted

Betz, H.D. *The Greek Magical Papyri in Translation: Including the Demotic Spells.* Chicago: The University of Chicago Press, 1986.

Copenhaver, Brian P. *Hermetica: The Greek Corpus Hermeticum and the Latin Asclepius in a New English Translation, with Notes and Introduction.* Cambridge: University Press, 1992.

Dornseiff, F. *Das Alphabet in Mystik und Magie* Leipzig: Verlag und Druck von B.G. Teubner, 1925.

Heidel, Alexander. *The Babylonian Genesis.* Chicago: The University of Chicago Press, 1952.
Kern, Otto. *Orpheus: Eine Religionsgeschichtliche Untersuchung.* Berline: Weidmannsche Buchhandlung, 1920.